MIRROR, SIGNAL, MOVE ON

EVAN VIAS

authorHOUSE®

AuthorHouse™ UK
1663 Liberty Drive
Bloomington, IN 47403 USA
www.authorhouse.co.uk
Phone: UK TFN: 0800 0148641 (Toll Free inside the UK)
         UK Local: 02036 956322 (+44 20 3695 6322 from outside the UK)

Published by AuthorHouse 10/08/2020

ISBN: 978-1-7283-5644-0 (sc)
ISBN: 978-1-7283-5645-7 (hc)
ISBN: 978-1-7283-5643-3 (e)

Print information available on the last page.

This book is printed on acid-free paper.

CONTENTS

OVERVIEW

We are born naked into this world, but we come a long way. The older you get, we have some choices to make and maybe become wiser from all the mistakes of the past. Depending on how well you have been brought up, you decide which way to turn at the cross road and still maintain values or create new ones.

Everyone has something about their past. It can either be a good experience or a learning experience. That depends on what it is and how it is looked upon. Prestigious, creative or whatever you want it to be, the question is 'Is Your Story Worth Telling?'

Without someone who's done it before, you can end up making crucial mistakes, but you have to be honest with yourself about the mistakes to move on. I have learnt over the years that the experience will get much, much easier *and* more satisfying once you are honest.

Sometimes lots of things get frequently overlooked and you ask yourself where the heck to get started!

Most of the time we end up getting a bit insecure about what happened or what we have experienced. You get bored, you stand, stretch, and brew yet another pot of coffee and end up failing before you finish.

Our head can sometimes be full of dreams even from an early age but unfortunately luck does not appear to be on your side despite your best efforts.

Any dreams you had about life, you can create for yourself. The only way it will take impact is the way you make it or want it to be and the sort of people that that you want to assemble around you and the difference you are willing to make in the world.

We all want to be the king or queen of our own manner, but this can be judged by our actions. We cannot change the past, but we can learn from it.

Over the years I have learned not to let fear talk me out of taking the risks that could really benefit me because I am not alone.

Emotions can be a power tool. Our mood determines how we interact with people round us, or how we deal with challenges and how we spend our time.

Gaining control over our emotions will help us become mentally stronger but we need to manage our emotions which requires practice and dedication.

Our human brain processes the experience of empathy, and it has the ability to understand another person's pain in a similar way to the experience of physical pain.

When we pray we focus on our healing, we are overcoming our strongholds and accomplishing things that others have found to be impossible to do. As amazing as this is, we need to understand that there are things to distract us from the task ahead and others will distract you or try to sit back and watch you win.

I have learned to reach out and try and get the vision of where and what I want to be. Taking a leap of faith.

ABOUT THE AUTHOR

The title of my book is Mirror, Signal, and Move on. We get and receive different signals of learning experiences so we can decide whether we should stay as we are or to move on. This what my book is all about. I am new writer and I was considering putting pen to paper for a few years about my story growing up as a child. During the Covid-19 lockdown, I found the time to compile my story into a book and I am hoping that my book will be able to transform your life.

This book is my memoir of a child growing up without any biological parents and living with strangers starting from an elderly couple who had no children of their own, then to a church minister, followed by travelling to a country with a different language to meet my sister for the first time.

I was raped and abused from an early stage by a female teacher. With no internet or counselling in the eighties, at first I did not understand what had happened or know who to talk to. It continued with others taking advantage of me so I started to believe it was the norm.

Later on I found out what happened with my biological mother from her best friend. I went through so many emotions when I heard the story but it gave me the sense that there was this larger world and processes that my existence was built upon. It was a way to help me understand myself and why I felt the way I did. This is something I will never forget.

Carrying these thoughts with me until today made me want to empower others with this book and maybe help them to overcome their own experiences as time passes.

INTRODUCTION

As I perched myself uncomfortably, restless on the bed, I started to fiddle with the sleeve of my knitted jumper and began to pull slowly at a piece of tread. Watching it get longer, I realised the jumper was unravelling.

Realising that once the thread has come loose, the jumper cannot be fixed. So I stopped and let go of the thread. Once changed, I cannot go back. The thread can or maybe re-sewn, but there is always a chance it will unravel again. Much like me.

Watching the drop of dew trickle down the window and come to a standstill, I turned to face the centre of my room, and grabbed a paper and pen, abruptly removing the lid from the pen and forced it onto the paper.

As I sit here to write, I believe that life is like a mirror. If you frown at it, it frowns back at you, but if you smile, it returns the greeting and that's the best result we can ever hope for.

This is something I wanted to do for a long time. As you may know, other things get into way, or become higher priority. I kept putting it off again and again, and I believe this is the right time.

Life is like a mirror, we can look at it in many ways. We look at ourselves from different angles and from different directions. We receive and send out signals and many may interpret it in which way we see best. Then we move in whatever direction life leads us.

I believe it is essential to help one another the best way possible and you are reading this book today because the chapters in this book can give you or someone else an overview of what they can learn or experience.

In this book I will be looking at our values, our beliefs, and our personality. What sort of roles we play in our society and with our family, our past memories, what our hopes for the future look like, as well as our hobbies and interests.

Everyone has a passion for something, and can show great potential and my passion is helping and sharing my expertise the best way I can without asking for anything including money. I class myself as a people person. I am a talker but never sat down and put pen to paper. People come to me for advice on different topics, and one of these topics is about my tests in life. Once I start talking I cannot stop, because of how much I love to share my experiences with others and I hope it will help them in their walks of life.

When I look into the mirror, I ask myself what do I see. Is everyone else seeing the same as what I see? Most of the time we can feel we are in the dark and all we can see is our reflections and in some cases it can be scary. But we have to pick ourselves up and take control and recognise it's me and do something about it.

Rejection can be part of life and in some cases you don't receive any response at all. I hope when you read this book, you will feel enthusiastic and it will inspire and uplift you in whatever way possible.

We've all been there at some point of our lives. I know I have. In some cases it was a bit of agonising over how to write this biography that doesn't sound too self-promotional or reveal too much of my modesty. So here in my biography it has a bit of a traditional format of me listing where I was and how I have accomplished the things in my life.

CHAPTER ONE

What's my Identity?

As we grow and develop from children to young adults, we listen to and learn from the world and the people around us. When others listen to and learn from us, we learn that our needs are valid and that we are valuable.

As a child growing up without my biological parents back in the seventies in South America, I had no idea if the people I was living with were my real parents. As I got older I started to realise that we were not related by blood, but I have accepted that they were my parents.

They were a married couple in their sixties but did not have any children of their own, so they accepted me as their own, and they showed me from an early stage what sort of responsibility I should have growing up. I want to say at this point that I thank them for the great upbringing. They have instilled some great values and beliefs which are reflected in my personality. They taught me the way I should be and behave and the role I should play in society and with whomever I come across in life. I knew for a fact that my hopes and future as well as my hobbies and interests would be bright.

I believe while growing up I was getting to know and understand myself. I think. But I was still looking for clues so I could start putting together the building blocks of myself. I had learnt a sense of self, but at times I relied on the opinions, feelings, and thoughts of others.

One of those clues for myself was 'happiness.' Being the only child in the family with no other siblings and living only with these two elderly parents was not easy, but I was grateful. The question was, what does a child have in common with elderly parents?

So from an early age I started expressing desires to experience more things. It was like when your outside actions are not in accordance with your inner feelings and values.

Looking in a mirror is often a transformative experience, but whether that transformation is positive or negative depends on so many factors, both external and internal. When I look into the mirror, what am I seeing? Is it the same as what other people are seeing? Am I recognising that the image I am seeing is mine? Sometimes I think I do know myself, but there is a conflict between myself and what I am seeing. Who is this person looking back at me?

I had lots of friends. There were some people who wanted to be my friend, and others whose friend I wanted to be. I learned from an early age to make choices about everything, including which company was not good for me. I wanted to be around people who understood me and could motivate me to resist bad habits and develop good ones. This was because of the values that were ground into me. I had the insight to know which values and goals I wanted to achieve, and I knew I had the power to do so.

One of my values is that I love helping others, putting others first. Maybe this value developed because I wanted others to start liking me. I needed something that would draw my attention over a sustained period of time. Helping others focuses my mental state. I am always seeing problems that I want to fix.

My feelings and body tell me a lot about my thoughts and interests. When I participate in activities such as sports or social events, I feel wanted and a part of the group. I start to laugh and feel happy and relaxed with the people around me.

When I begin to develop a sense of interest within the group

I am in, I feel wanted, and I begin to make decisions. I see it as an adventure of my life in discovering who I really am.

Making sense of my past

There are things which happen to us that define who we become, although we may not be able to make any sense of what's happened to us at the time.

When I was growing up, there was no social media. In those days more than ever we were called upon to show off 'who we were.' Socialising with friends encouraged the best of us to exaggerate our good bits while glossing over the bad. For some of us, our inability to be authentic was much like the online issues we have today.

My identity is the way I define myself. Some may like or love it; some may deny and reject it. My identity includes my values, my beliefs, and my personality. It also encompasses the roles I play in society and with family, my past memories, and my hopes for the future, as well as my hobbies and interests. Most of these things can, of course, affect my experience in life-changing circumstances.

Painful early life experiences often determine how I define and defend myself. In short, they can bend me out of shape, influencing my behaviour in ways which I am hardly aware of.

The attitude and atmosphere I experienced when I was growing up played a heavy hand on how I act as an adult.

Some treated me as someone special or as a unique gift; some created their own portrait of me as their friend and family because they wanted to see me in their character as a person. I started to believe that I was designed to be the person I wanted to be that my life was an incredible masterpiece.

I was raised in the church. That's all we had back in the seventies and eighties, and even back then that seed of a Christian value was planted within me. I knew that if I turned to God in prayer—which could mean simply talking and listening to him or writing to him in a journal—I could find myself being transformed from confusion to order, anxiety to serenity, and despair to hope. I also knew that this transformation was the will of he who sent me and 'It is the father living in me who is doing this work.'

I was the only child up to the age of three. Then my biological mother arrived one day out of the blue to visit these two lovely elderly people and brought with her a little baby girl which turned out to be my sister. It was like a delivery: drop off and go. She made lots of promises to return and support us, but that did not happen.

We discovered my sister had been born with a heart problem. Her heart was too small for her body. There was a lot of home care during her life. There was no one to play with because of her ill health, so I used to go out and play with my neighbour's children while my adopted mother cared for my sister.

As life went on her ill health became worse. My adopted mother did some investigation to find my biological mother, but instead she found my sister's biological father, who was very rich. He even had a street named after him.

He already had four grown sons, but only one was living with him. He heard that he had a daughter but couldn't find her anywhere. So when my adopted mother made contact, he was very happy to hear of his daughter and wanted to take on fatherly responsibility.

At this point it was a bit too late to do anything, as my sister's ill health had started to get even worse. He thought he would take on the responsibly because he had all the money. He took that responsibility and put all his energy to paying for her health as part of his solution to the problem. Despite concerns and recommendations from professionals, he did not realise it was a bit too late. She became seriously disabled. She had depression and was not able to walk.

She lived until the tender age of nine years. I was eleven at the time.

At this age I was trying to make sense of all this. One day I had a sister, then the next no more sister. There was the ever-present 'What happened?' Her death started to consume my every thought. Not only were we experiencing the shock; we also had the agony of not knowing what could have been done beforehand.

The grief that followed my sister's sudden death changed me, and for me, what followed was months of mixed emotions. Disbelief, agony, anger, and confusion.

While I did believe that her soul was now in heaven with the Lord, I wondered what she would think and how would she feel if she knew what I was doing. This was all-consuming, and still is today, even all these years later.

I started asking my friends in my community for suggestions for people who'd experienced the death of a sibling. Although some were able to make recommendations, many were quick to point out their struggle to find help and support for their loss.

It was hard for all of us, especially for her father. No doubt it was life-changing. And what next? Well, we'd been dreading December, of course. We knew it would remind us of the few months and years we shared together, especially birthdays and Christmases, the time of happiness and love and family and light. There was none of that for us without her. We would pretend, though. We had become good at that.

And what did I think about? I thought about how strange it was to suddenly be an only child. I thought about how little support there was out there for grieving siblings because the grieving parents often overshadowed them.

At a time when I felt the most lost and alone, I was expected to be strong for my adopted mother, to be there for her. When allowed, I did what I could.

Because I wasn't raised by my biological parents I had to grow up very quickly, not only to be the kind of man of the house, but also to help in any way possible and where I could.

After the death of my one and only sister, my adopted mother reached out and found my biological grandfather (my mother's father) who was living about five hours drive from where we were.

In those days there were no cell or mobile phones, it was either a house landline or a telegram. I was not sure how she got hold of him and what method she used, all I knew was there was some sort of contact and communication.

Everything seemed to be happening so quickly and I was very

5

surprised by the results. I even started to doubt whether this man was my grandfather and was it actually biological. As I did have doubts, it didn't come as too much of a surprise, but it still hit me hard. Even though I'd never met anybody from my father's side or my mother's side of the family.

We took a trip to see him and he was so happy and over-joyed to see me. I remember him saying to me "you are my one and only grandson" – "I heard of you". So I developed a connection with him, I was excited to see him too. I had no proof other than what they had told me, but deep down I knew it must be true.

I was given a surname that no one could explain. I didn't know whose name I was carrying so I told myself it must most likely be my biological grandfather. Then I found out it was not true. That didn't help me at all, even when I was trying to figure everything out. So assuming that all of this is indeed true, I had to just accept it and move on from there.

In those days there were no such thing as a DNA test, or computers with google search, so I had to accept everything everyone was telling me. Hey … I was very young, what did I know?

I did continue to visit him as often as possible when I could, especially in the school holidays with my adopted mother.

I loved getting to see and be around families. Every holiday I would go with my adopted mother to visit her family and after a week or so I would spend some of my holiday with my granddad. However, this time around, the holiday was more special to me than any other time I had been there.

When I visited my granddad, I saw this woman. She came up to me and said 'hello – I am your aunty'. I stood there not knowing what to say. I became so silent.

My granddad told me even before I opened my mouth, because the silence was killing him. He said 'I want you to meet your aunt for the first time'. I was so emotional. I wanted to cry with happiness because family was so important to me. Just knowing that I had a whole family coming together that I had never seen before made me happy.

No one spoke about the past. Not even my aunt spoke about her sister (my mother). In fact, I didn't know what on earth was going on. All of a sudden it seemed as if they were talking a different language, because I did not understand anything, and no one was willing to explain any of it to me.

She showed me a picture of a man, and said 'this picture of this person is your biological father' – I said 'OK.' I was taking everything in as so many things were happening all at the same time, and maybe it was getting too much for me.

She continued by saying 'your father is a very rich man' - 'he already has his family.'

Now I had just discovered that I was a child outside of someone's happy marriage. Even worse, I couldn't see him or the family, so I was now the hidden child from his family's house.

What was even more confusing is that it seemed as if this family had been in on it as well and they themselves didn't even know about me. It seems like I was the ignorant person in every family I had come across so far.

Someone needed to be honest with me so that I knew exactly what was going on. Then I could decide on my future – with or without any of these people I needed to make a decision or someone needed to suggest what I must do. But no one came forward with any decision or suggestion and I couldn't make any informed decisions about my biological family and how to solve the problem.

My aunt told me that if my biological father knew about me, he would claim that I was not his child, all because that will break up his family. I was not sure if I was getting angry or confused so I asked "What should I do"?

Later on I realised that I wasn't going to get anywhere with this and now I had no one to help me. All everyone was telling me was the history.

Time and things started to change, I started to focus on challenging stigma and discrimination in this small town as my adopted mother started to suffer from mental illness. At that tender age I was not able to provide any individual support and there was no emergency support for people like her in crisis.

The minister of the church tried his best to provide some kind of confidential, non-judgmental emotional support for her and for me, as I was experiencing the feelings of distress and despair.

With all the support and understanding, things can happen in life that enables people to make informed choices. But there was not much or any kind of information on types of mental health problems, where to get help, drug treatments, alternative therapies and advocacy at the time.

It came to a point by which I had to take on most of the responsibly of the home as things started to get a bit worse. Some days I struggled to fulfil my responsibilities. This is something I did not anticipate, but I had to increase my work rate to help the best way I knew how.

I did not want anyone outside the house to know what was happening within our home or to my adopted mother. I would make sure that my room and the house were tidy and clean. I cleaned up any mess as soon as possible. I made sure that there was always clean pillowcases, sheets, and blankets on the bed at least once a week to keep everything fresh and clean and I put the rubbish out, and emptied it before it started to overflow.

My adopted mother would sometimes appreciate my help but it wasn't just her job to keep the household running smoothly. It was mine as well because with the way things were, I had to take on that responsibility of the household, right down to very basic chores.

Every day when I woke up I didn't know how to overcome the everyday difficulties I would face.

My job revolved around helping my adopted mother with her immediate needs such as washing, dressing and maintaining her hygiene, as well as helping her with her basic day-to-day administrative tasks like paying bills.

I must say I was probably the only companion she had as well as taking on the duties and responsibilities of being her carer. I had to learn the knowledge and skills of a carer at a young age.

Things started to take another turn. My dear adopted mother

was diagnosed with dementia but I had no idea what that meant or what it would mean as time went on. I was living with her and seeing all these changes as the days and months went on. It was becoming clear or even clearer that I could take care of her and she wanted it to stay that way.

Once the diagnosis was made, the doctors and specialist psychiatrist came and visited with her a couple of times – but then we were on our own. There was no further follow-up.

I tried so hard to listen and understand what was going on and what I could do to help, then found out much later that the doctor should have referred us for some kind of family support. But that didn't happen in our case, so I was just waiting for the crisis to become worse every day when I wake up.

It was a struggle to go to school. There were no mobile phones back in those days. All we had was an old fashion home telephone so I was terrified that something would happened to her if I left the house, even to play with my friends.

I started to become very exhausted and I didn't want to go away from the house so my friends will come over and play with me. They were sympathetic whenever I needed to deal with a crisis – of which there were a few.

Looking back, I remember often thinking that she was being difficult or belligerent as I had no idea that she had dementia or what that really meant. It was very confusing.

She obviously knew that something was wrong and she had ways of covering up her own confusion, batting away any queries from me very convincingly. I learned later that this is classic of the early stages of dementia, well … … that is what they told me. It must have been frightening for her – not understanding what was happening.

I couldn't concentrate on school or anything else, as I was constantly worrying about her. I couldn't plan anything … just in case. She herself was bored and miserable and confused. Finding out 'what happens now?' was also a test for me. Days stretched into weeks and I could see weeks stretching into months.

Alongside all the mental stress and the time-consuming nature of dealing with the 'problem', I was also losing my adopted mum.

Dementia was – and continued – to erase her. I didn't have time to enjoy being the son with her. I was grieving for her constantly. I was grieving for the loss of her for quite a few months, until I came to terms with what the process of dementia is and what it robs you of.

Along with that I was aware that my time with a hands-on mum was also diminishing. I had lost some of my mum, but I hadn't lost all of her. She is still there. Her hand felt the same as it always did when I held it. The cheek that I kissed was still the same soft cheek I always enjoyed being close to.

She hugs me tight and I feel like her little boy … still, because my little sister is no longer around. I am grateful that I have got to this point with her and that we still have some time left to enjoy together. In fact, now that I don't have to worry if she has locked her doors, or paid her bills, or turned off her gas hob, or has eaten some food, when I do see her I can genuinely just enjoy being with her.

I happened to be getting mum ready for bed and found her bra was inside out. I checked it. I tried my best to fix it and put it on the correct way. I had no idea what to do with a bra or even what my mum's bra size was – who does? I had to run to the shop and back again to get a measuring tape and went out the next day and bought her some new underwear. This may be a small thing, but to me it was important. I wanted everything as much as possible to be how mum would want it to be. I tried to keep an eye on the small stuff

Care is a funny old word, though. I think anyone can provide care, but not many provide compassion. I was lucky that my mum was now somewhere with her family and where her family were able to look after her in a genuinely compassionate and empathetic way. I wanted this because I loved her so much.

CHAPTER TWO

Taking life to another level

It took a long while before I realized it wasn't good enough simply to endure life. I had to learn to live again. I made some new choices. I needed to do whatever was needed to take my life to the next level.

I believed that God was moving me to another level and I was about to move forward. God wanted to use me from where I was. And I could feel within my spirit that God wanted to increase that. I was willing to receive that increase!

There was a new minister who came to the church, he was a professor and worked part time at the University of Guyana, but he was the full time minister.

He knew that caring for an elderly person at this tender age, was not the life for me. So he came up with this suggestion. It was hard to accept but I had no choice.

I wanted to explore what life was all about. So I decided and felt encouraged to stay with the minister of my church. My adopted mother had to go to the east coast to stay with her family as I couldn't do much for her.

I moved in with him because I spent quite a bit of time talking about dealing with Father Hunger. There was so much more I wanted to do with a father figure. I could spend hours talking about important issues.

I got myself involved with many things within the church. As you can imagine, living with a minister, everyone started to believe that I was his son. I learnt to play the piano and other musical instruments, became part of the church choir and other stuff so I could help out in the church.

I know for a fact that there were many kids my age who were without a father. Many young men grow up with absent fathers. Some of my friends' dads were physically absent, others were emotionally so and some were distracted from their children by work, their own grief, rage or substance misuse. They spent little real quality time with them, and when they did, still spent time at other places or other distractions from intimacy, rather than actually engaging emotionally or listening to their children.

In my heart I was grateful that I met this minister as a father figure. My adopted mother would be better looked after with her family as the situation was getting too much for me at this tender age and I believed that things would improve for her and that I would be able to visit her as often as I could.

Her symptoms were manageable enough so that they could keep caring for her and there were more opportunities for her to be on her own. I knew that getting used to these differences would take time, but I believed things would get much smoother for me in the long run.

I needed to understand the biggest challenge I had to face in my lifetime. But at this crucial moment I had to grow up quickly and learn what life was there ahead of me.

I had to factor in some sort of order of 'most important' to 'least important.' The first thing on the minister's list was a good education as he believed that was the best chance to get ahead in life. He wanted to ensure that I did not miss out on any opportunities of life, no matter where or what I was, I must have the best possible opportunities.

I started to attend school again and on top of that I started to do some extra stuff such as learning to type and shorthand. It was called pitman's typewriting then.

I started to enjoy it which meant I was no longer clinging to a life that was devoid of meaning but I soon felt a bit lost. I started struggling to forge a new path for myself, even if that path wasn't crystal clear yet.

Maybe or perhaps I was comparing it to the split second where I had to let go of the company of friends I started to be part of. It felt a bit terrifying and felt like a freefall at the time, but in reality, it's just a necessary component of moving forward.

I spent a lot of time getting to know myself as an independent person – understanding what I wanted, what I was capable of and what I had to give back to others. And the fact that I was craving the company of others meant I was finally feeling ready to open myself back up to people – to invest in others and to start building new relationships in a healthy way as I felt like and was a lonely child with no siblings.

I had been alone for a long time, and I was growing tired of it.

I learnt quickly that I had to face any fear at this early stage of my life and I was and still am motivated and prepared to face the challenges. There were times when external forces took control, but I hated to give in to temptation, especially listening to anyone with an opinion that I did not agreed with.

Okay yes, so failure sucks. There's no great way to sugar coat it. But the fact that I've recently failed at a new endeavour goes to show that I am always willing trying for new things – instead of getting stuck in the same old habit patterns.

Being disappointed with myself means I was refusing to see myself as a victim – I was recognising the ways in which I could improve and understanding that those opportunities for change lie within myself, not outside of myself.

Last Generation

Life then was very different than today. Although some things have not changed, other aspects of life then are unrecognisable today.

Every generation has their stories about what it was like to grow up in their day. Back in those days people talked about how they had to walk everywhere; and I know it was all true, because I had to do the same. I had to walk miles and miles just to go everywhere and my school was about a mile away which I had to do every day. Most people didn't have a lot back then.

Growing up during that period was not easy, but as a child it was fun. Everything was rationed. We had to ration everything and we planted our own crops to put food on the table. During the political system of that time, things were very tough even to afford to buy everyday things like sugar and gas. Unfortunately we did not have a luxurious lifestyle. We had to make our own bread from rice. Living such a life has affected almost everything in our lives today.

I began to focus on healthy living and trying something new by learning something new. Also, I had learnt to build relationships with others in the community where I was. I had respect, and knew how to look after myself but most of the time I had no idea about technology. The only technology we had was the typewriter and the radio. In our home there was no television until later on but it had a positive impact and we managed to do just about everything. Whenever we wanted to know about something, we looked it up in the public library or we used magazine articles or the newspaper. This is how we could learn everything about anything that was known at the time.

Long before things such as Spotify, mp3's or peer to peer file sharing existed I had to either save up some money to buy official copies of songs or tape them off the radio. I would spend hours waiting for that one particular tune to play and hurried to press the record button in time.

Sometimes I was 'thrown a bone' and could tape the latest charts, but for those less popular tunes, I had to put in the effort. This led to the satisfaction of perfectly timing it to cut out the DJ's, often inane, contributions.

I had to get off my backside and leave the house for shopping which meant I had to walk to the local store or the central market.

Watching a movie required me to go (and pay) at a cinema and I would actually meet and make friends with people in person.

These were dark times when I needed to actually search and read through reams of text for the information I was after. How things have changed! Of course, it had its benefits. It would take an equally incredible amount of effort for someone to check any statements of fact if not common knowledge - which was handy at times.

There's a saying that goes like, 'when I was in my teens, it seemed to me that those who turned thirty are already old.' As I grew older, things really changed. It's not just about the appearance, but also about how I treated my health, my family and friends, my money, and other things. What was significant in our teens becomes not such a big priority when we turn thirty, and vice versa.

I was born into a generation and grew up in the seventies. We had and did the craziest things back then, which meant we had to ask all the hard, embarrassing questions in person. Life was fascinating before all the stuff we have today. It was filled with things I could hear, see, touch, smell and taste.

When there was nothing to, I had to find something semi-productive to do. In other words, when there were no friends to hang out with, or anywhere fun to go, I was forced to do things like read, write, paint, exercise, and other productive things like that. My entire weekends couldn't be spent on the couch binge-watching any favourite shows.

Many jobs taken for granted today didn't exist back then before the internet. If you'd mentioned you were a web designer, people would look at you strangely. After all the only things that 'designed' webs were spiders right? Life after the internet would never be the same again.

Office life before the internet was a lot harder than today. If I wanted to look at cute cat pictures, and still look like I was working, would have been tough to pull off! Procrastination has never been easier - aren't we lucky?

Life changes

The typewriting school I was attending was full of women and I was the only boy within the whole school. There was no one there of my age.

I had now become the centrepiece of the school. Everyone wanted to be with me. Maybe they saw me as cute and maybe good looking.

The teacher who was in charge was a good looking woman with a husband but no children as they were recently married. One day she said to me 'what do you want to be in the future' I said 'not sure as yet but I want to be successful.' In return she said 'you say you want success, so what are you doing about it? Don't say you're serious about success and then you don't take consistent action.'

So I thought OK that means she is giving me some good advice.

She said 'people invest more time in failure then they do in success, success is reserved for those who put in the effort to make their dreams come true.' I said 'OK – what do I need to do?' She said 'I will teach you – just follow my lead.'

To be honest, I wasn't too sure what that really meant, but it sounded very exciting and I was ready to give it a go, because it seemed like she knew what she was talking about, so maybe I could learn something.

I was ready to live life to the limit, to learn something and have that life of my dreams.

One day I was preparing for one of my typewriting exams and she looked at me and said 'if you are struggling, I can help' so I said 'no it's OK.' I got up and went to the toilet. She saw me going to the toilet so she got up and started walking behind me. I didn't think anything of it. Next thing I knew she was behind me in the toilet.

She locked the door, I was so shocked I forgot what I went in the toilet for. She grabbed me, lifted me up and pinned me to the wall. She wrapped her legs around my waist with her hands moving slowly towards my head and then all the way to my private parts.

I was not sure what was happening, as this was my first time such a thing ever happened to me, but desire stirred within me.

'Stop I said' as I struggled.

Her moving all over me didn't help me or with my mini me. She pinned me harder to the wall, and said 'lesson one, to be successful - this is how you kiss.' She began to moan as she continued to nuzzle my neck. I didn't know what to do. I started shaking and she kept saying to me 'it will be OK – don't worry.' There was a knock on the door. She then covered my mouth with her hands and said 'tell that person you'll be out in a second.' She said 'end of lesson one' as she pulled me closer and kissed me on my neck.

Not sure how I felt at the time.

That feeling and experience of that kiss was so powerful it made me feel like two souls united as two lovers. It represents one of the most delightful things that has ever happened to me for the first time in my life.

Although there was no sex, she just played with my mini me, it gave me that devoted attention and the meaning and the importance of kissing and what it felt like to get that attention stayed with me for a long time.

It moved me from adolescence into adulthood even at that young age.

But how did I feel at that moment after that actual first kiss on my lips. Not sure. Was I excited and happy? Or anxious and worried?

It was a little surprising, but it was an experience I will never forget. I was young. Just hitting my teenager years and there were things that I found confusing about sex … things that boggled my mind about how a woman who could be my mother thinks and operates.

I asked myself so many different questions after that event in the toilet over the next few days trying to understand girls or women and what she wanted from me. It was that one area that caused me a lot of anxiety.

After everything was done. I returned to my desk and continued my work and tried to keep a straight face as if nothing happen. The following day I went back to finish the second part of preparation for my exams and she came over to me and said 'I will help you with your exam because I want you to help me with something'

I said 'OK'

Late that evening when everyone was leaving she said 'we need to talk.' So in return I said 'OK.' Maybe all the words I had in my head at the time was 'OK.' That evening it was time to close the building. She held my hands and took me into a small room which was next to her office.

This is where she opened up to me and told me about her husband. She said to me on that late evening 'I am being open with you but at the same time I am vulnerable. I keep everything locked inside. I keep all my feelings and thoughts to myself, as I am kind of emotional right now. … I can't trust anyone and I am feeling empty.'

I was sitting opposite her, listening to every word that was coming out of her mouth. Emotionally, I was finding myself somewhere in the middle of the road, far from either ditch. Somehow I had a feeling that this woman was looking for some kind of companion and the more she spoke, my body was kind of getting a bit cold and this deep affection for this woman started to overcome me.

She said 'I really appreciate you listening to me and that really means a lot to me. I trust you.'

With those kinds of words, I found myself holding her hands gently and carefully as she was opening up and sharing her heart with me. I believed I was giving her a sign of trust. I think at the time it was trust that was a valuable quality. I started taking an interest in what was going on with the details of her life, and saw how she responded just by holding her hands.

The next thing I know and remember was I was naked and she was all over me saying 'don't worry it will be fine'

There is where I learnt very quickly that sex drive is complex and is affected by your physical and emotional state and is not just for procreation—it can also be pleasurable. The sex you hear about from other people, what you see on TV or in magazines or maybe learn in school is not as accurate as it could be. It was not until I had experienced it that day for the first time of my life that I realised this.

On that evening she treated me like an adult and coaxed me to take the lead as we both played a sexual game.

She said 'this is what is missing'

At that moment I was feeling traumatised. At the time she made me feel happy, smiley and warm inside. Maybe this was because I needed some attention or maybe I was grateful and thankful for the attention. I don't know.

How can somebody be doing wrong when it makes me feel like that? 'I loved being with you and hope you are feeling the same way' she said. I was afraid to speak to anyone about what had just happened.

My mind was racing away with so many things going around in my head. But I kept telling myself that there was someone who needed some loving and attention like myself and maybe the person to provide it was me.

That evening I could feel my sweat running down me unto her and she didn't mind, and that night before I went to bed I looked into the mirror at myself thinking was this a nightmare? When I got into bed, I told myself 'yes you're right, it did happen.' It was so real, it took me a few minutes to clear it from my mind so I could sleep.

What did I know about sex at this early and tender age? But something was telling that this wasn't right. I kept telling myself there must be more to sex than putting my mini me into her. But to make her happy (I think) I decided to keep doing it with her and do my best to keep it simple and just focus on what she wants. It was more an enjoyable experience for her than me.

This continued for about two months.

I moved to another school to learn a technical computing IT skill, which was a major step for me back in the late eighties and early nineties. I was doing well for the first few months, until some of the girls in the school (not only my class) wanted to be friends with me.

Once I started to get that attention, I started having fantasies about the girls who needed my attention. The good news was they were about my age. I knew that I had my secret - and I liked it that way. Sure, I thought I will try something different, but I had no idea how to make it happen, and didn't really expect it to.

At first, it reminded me that some of these girls needed my attention and I was loving the attention I was getting, and at least one or more of them could fancy me. It was strange, but it was the comforting way to get back in the game; swiping through pictures in my head without having to engage with anyone until I felt ready.

One thing I did know for sure, I didn't have to worry or wonder what it'd be like to sleep with a woman - so I decided to live out my sex fantasy and it was so empowering.

Every time one of them got too close to me like giving me a hug I realised women's bodies turned me on. One day I decided to be a gentleman and walked one of the girls in my school (not my class) home, knowing full well it would be a long way back to my home. But I wanted to impress her.

When we arrived at her place no one was home. She said that she was going to get some water for a bath. She went and got the water and I could see her from where I was sitting. The bedroom did not have a door, there was only a piece of cloth hanging up. As I sat there looking at her I saw that she was undressing herself and it was like she wanted me to see her. I heard something drop very hard on the floor so I got up and went to have a look and to make sure she was OK.

When I got into the room she was totally naked and she said 'I am in that mood' I said 'what mood' knowing full well what she was talking about. Of course that excited me. I decided that for the next few minutes I had to do something before anyone else of the house came home. What happened next was incredible for both of us participating. It seemed as if she found that happiness and fulfilment that I was having too.

I did not know the direct correlation between 'nice guys' and the friend-zone. These girls in this school just thought I was a nice guy. Well … … in my head. Or maybe they saw me as an ultimate challenge, a challenge to get and a challenge to keep. Why … … maybe they saw in me a person with a dysfunctional dating lifestyle or some bizarre creature, and the reason I knew that was because I started to feel like I was becoming one.

Doing the 'right' thing might sound great, but it sends instant signals to women that you lack spontaneity and that you over-analyse situations rather than acting on raw instinct.

One thing I learnt very quickly that 'word travels fast', and if a woman knows that you want a girlfriend then you lack the challenge and appeal that all women are drawn to. The next day going back to school, I learnt that the news travels fast. I wasn't too sure how much details were said, but I had that constant feeling of guilt afterwards because there was a little bit of fire and drama in the school ground.

I went to hang out with the boys, but I could feel and see all the eyes of the girls on me. It was obvious that everyone could see how flustered I was. So I made up my mind I was not moving from where I was until it was time to go back into the school or home.

I believe I am a dynamic and a charismatic person, I have it all under control. Of course, I realised 'I didn't want to hurt anyone's feelings.'

After a few months I started to have more feelings for her but the relationship that began with great potential came to an unexpected end. It took roughly a week of processing through, journaling and reflection to finally be at peace with it. Just know that my takeaway was that it was a beautiful experience where two people became closer in the stages of getting to know one another. That ended with me walking her home for the last time and us sharing a goodnight kiss.

Somehow, though, we kept talking when we were at school. Instead of ending the conversation I stayed on and stood there in front of her with discomfort. Before long we were onto a different topic and chatting away. This was good, though.

Adolescent Rebellion

As the years and months went by, and as I got a bit older, I started to become this caricature of the teenager. Adolescent rebellion. This started to cause, let's say a bit of conflict with the minister.

I was becoming this rebellious child who was against socially fitting in and against adult authority - non-compliance. This rebellion was attracting everyone's attention. Let's put it this way: This young teenager person proudly asserts individuality from what the elders like or independence from what elders want, and in each case succeeds in provoking their disapproval.

I found a brilliant way to meet new people; well … some in my age group and to make lots of new friends very quickly in what I called a relaxed safe and friendly atmosphere. I started to go out to night clubs, and the club atmosphere was getting very exciting and there I quickly became part of the night club family.

I started to choose from a wide range of activities or social events to get out more because I though this may be a brilliant way to make new friends as I believed sharing my experiences with others would be the best ice breaker.

The emphasis was always to have a great time with like-minded people my age. So like most of us, I picked up my strategies from similar confused young men around me. Even though that's pretty normal, in terms of instructions on how to be a mature and respectful person it was easy to do worse than that – so I was hoping I could offer something to fit in with the others and that would be OK among my peers.

I was getting to be this perpetually busy person who always had something to do and people to meet, looking for the next function, or social engagement. Of course, I was lying all the time to the minister just to get out of the house or finding any excuse for me to get up to my antics. I would lie so much because I knew that if I told the truth, none of this was going to happen. All I would have got was a long sermon about what I should or should not do. Once I was out of the house it was a way to meet up with friends, and that was a sigh of relief that I had lied again, then later I would think about it and tell myself how 'disappointed' I am with myself and the dreadfulness of my character. I couldn't tell an elaborate lie. The lie had to be small and something I won't have to remember or keep up for days and weeks. I tried keeping the information to a minimum, so he couldn't ask lot of questions.

I saw this girl come into the main entrance of the nightclub who was so beautiful but she was a bit older than me. I kept looking at her trying to see if she was with anyone. But all night she was alone with her girlfriends having fun. I turned my chair where I was sitting and drinking so I could keep looking at her. It was like I was her bodyguard.

I was sitting there thinking of a smooth opening line. I looked in my pocket to see how much money I had, but unfortunately it was not enough to buy her a drink as I had spent all my money earlier. My friend who was sitting next to me, noticed what was happening and he said, 'would you like to borrow some money?' I said 'nah, I am good'

Five minutes later, I said 'go on I will take it' because I couldn't let this beautiful woman get away and slip through my fingers. I plucked up the courage and went over to her and introduced myself and the first thing she said to me was 'wow … you are handsome' I said 'thank you and you are beautiful' – I don't know where those words came from. The conversation flowed like a river and the time felt right with the smoothness of words that were coming out of my mouth, I was starting to believe this could be the match of a life-time for me.

Getting through the awkwardness into boldness I could feel the sweet taste of victory being abolished by a sinking feeling in my stomach. Meeting this girl for the first time was different, I could feel this was different. I started to feel some butterflies, I asked myself is it normal to feel like this? – is this what they called love?

With that being said, I definitely didn't want to show that I was feeling nervous or panicky so I was making sure I was behaving like a man to ensure I was making a great first impression for this first time meeting her.

She had these lips and this body for any man to die for. There's nothing quite like the first kiss, it was like heaven just opened. At first looking at her and her lips was a bit nerve-wracking but the moment that I found that opportunity by getting closer to her, I went for it and I must say it was incredible and so worth it.

She was sophisticated, stunningly beautiful and seemed beyond my reach. She was five years older than me, but then it did not seem to be a problem. I chased her everywhere she went that night for a long time and as I was lucky enough to walk her home, I was able to treat her to all kinds of attention. She was very wary at the time, saying that the age difference was too much and she was worried that she would regret it later. I brushed all this off as I was blindingly in love and eventually, when we got to her place, she invited me in and that is when I hit the jackpot. We had sex; it was the most amazing sex of my life. We were at it like rabbits all night. I was over the moon.

She said to me that 'I am an old man in a young man's body.' If you are anything like me then you know what it's like to be singled out because of your maturation level. Being too mature for my age had several pros and cons and that came with some struggles of being level-headed.

This was probably one of the most difficult parts about being mature. Everyone wants to fit in and feel like they belong, but if your maturity surpasses that of your peers, then it became really difficult. I knew I was too mature for my age when I was in elementary school. I would hang around the teachers instead of interacting with the other young people like myself; I really just felt out of place when I did. It was safe to say that I related to older people more than I did to people my age. This was especially difficult when I was in college because everyone was hanging out with their friends and going to events, but I still felt alone because no one in the crowd was on my level.

I hate to say it, but yes it was true. Most people my age were very annoying to me due to their lack of maturity. Many conversations and behaviours that people my age had were just not appealing to me. Gossiping all day and standing up at the same house parties were not my thing, so yeah, it was frustrating when I knew I was the mature one.

She loved my maturity. We had a relationship for a few months. I wanted to be a gentleman and I saw this as a real love relationship with her. It meant being able to enjoy the instant gratification that comes with the romance of the moment while knowing the best is yet to come and being patient while I watched my love grow toward her. Showing her my unconditional love and hoping it will present itself in the relationship and would mature with time.

One evening I went to look for her at her place, but she wasn't home. I went to her school the following day and she wasn't there. It's a small town so I knew that she had to be somewhere. A few days later I saw her with another guy walking hand in hand. I started to become a stalker. My actions started to become unwelcome, unwanted, and downright creepy. I saw all the grand gestures that was going on with both of them. It was easy to be confused by their actions that I was seeing. They both were demonstrating publicly that intense, special love which I thought we had together. But this stalking was becoming a bit less about love and more about obsession and control. I was so heart broken.

I confronted her about what was going on. And she said to me clearly, 'sorry I am now with someone else' I did not see that coming. I even questioned my sanity. A few months in this relationship wasn't long, but I thought it was serious. I was so in love with the girl. This was my ever first serious relationship. Well … that is what I was thinking. That day I was feeling worse than ever before.

Breakups are emotional roller coasters. Actually that's not true. If a breakup was anything like a roller coaster the end would be visible from the start, but I definitely didn't see that. I felt like breakups were more like being under a roller coaster. The emotional pain of this breakup came with the physical pain and I thought that we both had something in common.

Being mentally strong isn't about me stifling my emotions and ignoring my pain. After all, it takes strength to allow myself to feel sad, anxious, and scared. I didn't want to stay stuck in a place of pain however. It was important to be able to shift my emotions when they weren't serving me well. I had learnt very quickly even at that age that if I put a lid on a boiling pot, eventually the contents will rise to the top and spill over and my emotions were no different. If I started pushing my feelings down and down and trying to avoid them, eventually they will explode out more fiercely than before.

I started to find things to occupy my mind. The goal of this was to contain my worrying to a specific portion of the day so it wasn't all consuming. With practice, I was be able to spend my day focusing on the task right in front of me, rather than ruminating about what happened yesterday or worrying about what might happen tomorrow.

CHAPTER THREE

Expect the Unexpected

Considering all possible scenarios is the solution for a lifestyle without disappointment.

I don't have an archive of a yearly routine, but over the years, I have forgotten almost all the mottos I have heard and learn, except one — a very classic motivational one but not that mainstream —

"expect the unexpected."

To me, of course, it is exactly the opposite. Instead of thinking only about the same thing all the time, I'd rather move in another direction. I definitely prefer diagonal or horizontal moves or even completely changing dimensions.

Another point is that my views on things are strongly connected with the feeling of what I deserve.

I expect this because I deserve it.

Lots of times I couldn't imagine how my life would unfold. Sometimes you can create a wonderful plan, complete with well-defined dots, connected by entirely straight lines. I soon realised that the map I drew in my mind was sketched in pencil, not in ink.

Looking into the future, it seemed that my life would unfold in predictable ways. Events would always be within my control. I tried so hard not to let myself be caught off guard. I expected difficulty and opportunity to arise but I had confidence that with my efforts and talents, I would turn straw into gold.

To get some additional perspective on this, I asked myself one simple question 'What was the biggest surprise in your life'? Most of the time I would receive a wide range of responses. Some of it could be heart-warming and positive. Others were tender and painful.

If there was one lesson that I took away from my previous responses it was that we all think that our lives are the only ones that took a winding path. The truth is that the opposite is true. We can all find comfort in the fact that everyone, just like us, is doing the best they can to deal with the surprises that life throws their way.

The minister I was staying with had a large congregation and one of his members who was close to my adopted mother, (as it was a small community and everyone knew each other) travelled to a nearby country for a short holiday. On her return she came to the church one Sunday and said to me.

'Hello how are you?'

I said 'I am fine, thank you'

She said 'I have some kind of good news for you'

I said 'really?'

She said 'you have a sister, who lives with her father in the neighbouring country'

I didn't know how to respond to this good news. In my head I was thinking of so many things. I didn't know if I should sit or remain standing. Was it a shock or a surprise?

She continued by saying that 'her family would like to meet you' as he handed me a letter. I tried so hard to show a positive and enthusiastic response to this happiness I was feeling.

She then spoke to the minister and shared the good news. The minister was at this point busy greeting his flock of people after the service.

To be honest I was worried what the minister would say. He looked surprised but he looked at me and smiled and I thought 'wow … I really misread his reaction.' The reason why was I knew that he did his best to raise me as his son because he did not have any son of his own. And of course he was like a father to me.

Perhaps I was thinking that he might be thinking I was going to be ungrateful for all he has done for me after my adopted mother went away.

Some of the most worthwhile things in life aren't easy. One of the things I like the most is "the power of positive thinking" and I believe I had that from the beginning and from an early age.

Over the years, I started to believe the implication that if you just have the right attitude and the right state of mind, the rest will just fall into place. In some cases and from experience, it can cause a lot of hurt and disappointment in people who invest their time, effort, and of course, money in someone's life and find themselves, a few years down the line, exactly where they were before, or not where they want to be.

I don't think that ultimately, God or the Spirits or the Universe or the world "provides". I think a lot of the time, the world puts obstacles in our way, and no amount of positive thinking makes them go away.

He had time to think about this news we both heard. He did not say anything to me for that evening. The next morning we saw each other at the dinner table having breakfast and he asked me 'what do you think about that?'

I said 'I don't know'

He said 'do you want to go and see your sister?'

I said 'I would like to'

He said 'where did this sister appear from?' and 'did you know about this?'

My honest reply was 'NO'

Meeting a sister you never knew you had for the first time can be the most magical moment. This can be rife with emotions, but I think it's a moment worth capturing regardless of the reaction.

The minister wrote a letter to the family, asking for more information. Within a couple of weeks we received a reply with an invitation to my sister's tenth birthday celebration which was a couple of months ahead.

The minister said 'What is more important than a relationship with your sibling?' He was being enthusiastic because something good had just happened to the son he never had who was now preparing to leave.

He said that he wasn't sure about this family and he didn't trust these people. His intrusive thoughts were unwanted thoughts that caused me a bit of distress and started to disturb me. It began to even make me worried that I was becoming this terrible and ungrateful person, but I believed that I was capable of doing things that go against my character.

All the recurrent and persistent thoughts, urges, and the images he was painting about this family started to have some sort disturbance in my thinking with intrusive and inappropriate thoughts and that caused me a bit of anxiety and distress.

I was a good listener, yet I often failed to believe what he was saying. I told myself 'Just keep listening.' I didn't interrupt with my own advice or allow myself to be distracted by other things.

He knew that he needed to be supportive because I was a lonely child. And I was hoping that he would support me and encourage me and not be cold-hearted towards me and in return for me to try not to feel bitter towards him if he didn't.

One day I stood in front of the mirror for a few minutes, it was not only a case of vanity. I looked for my own reflection because it was my unique way of talking to myself. Every time I can see myself in a reflection or a mirror it started to feed my own ego. I don't give myself a lot of value, sometimes even no value at all. I tried to assured myself that I did have some sort of value. It was this value I wanted to see in the mirror for myself and not have to wait for someone to tell me that. This enabled me to arouse respect and the admiration of others.

The instincts, attitudes and physical strengths he had helped to empower in me to be that tough-minded person, he also demonstrated in himself so he thought he had to make that sacrificial service towards me for me to meet with this family.

There have been many times in my life where I have been stuck, not having anyone to talk to or having any other siblings to share my thoughts with and not knowing what to do next. I have agonised over what I should do or not do and whether I was making the right choices.

This state of not knowing what to do next started to take its toll on me, and believe you me it can happen to all of us. It doesn't matter at what age you are, and trust me it can happen at different stages of our lives.

Whether I was heading off to university, graduating, choosing my own career path, recovering from a heartbreak or being made redundant from a family I never had in the first place, it came to a point in my life where I didn't know what to do next.

By not expecting what would happen it was time to make a decision. I felt it was time to put my running shoes on and clear my mind. At one time in my life, it was very challenging and emotional; all I could do was think about what I needed to do to get to the next day. I was getting a bit confused. One day I was very excited, the other days there were no thoughts of what I wanted to do in the future nor were there any thoughts of how I wanted my life to be. It was just a matter of surviving, praying and hoping from one day to the next.

One thing for sure was that waking my conscious mind was to accept my reality, embrace the change and the unpredictability of my life and there was one step toward finding out what I needed to do next in my life.

CHAPTER FOUR

The journey

Life is a journey. As a very small child I do not remember much, but the things that I do remember the most were seen through a child's eyes. This has made me the person that I am today, starting from my adopted mother and all the way through. I will always have those memories with me until my last breath on this earth.

Being faced with many different journeys, ups and downs, and obstacles at an early age, I didn't really think my life would go by in a blink of an eye ... wow, I was about to grow up very quickly.

The mind of a person is filled with the unknown, adventures waiting to be had and places waiting to be explored. Sometimes, I just needed a few words of extra encouragement to help me take that trip of a lifetime.

My life was and is a journey filled with lessons, hardships, heartaches, joys, celebrations and special moments that can and will ultimately lead me to my destination and my purpose in life. I have learnt that the road will not always be smooth; in fact, throughout my journey, I have encountered many challenges.

Some of these challenges on my journey have put me to the test, but I have learnt that it has given me the courage, strength, weaknesses, and faith to carry on. Along the way, I have stumbled upon obstacles that have come between the paths that I have been destined to take.

Along my journey I have been confronted with many situations, some of which have be filled with joy and some have been filled with heartache. The way I chose to react to what I have been faced with has determined what kind of outcome the rest of my journey through life was going to be like.

When things don't always go the way I wanted it to, I have two choices in dealing with the situations. Focus on the fact that things didn't go how I had hoped they would and let life pass me by, or two, I could make the best out of the situation and know that these are only temporary setbacks and find the lessons that I am willing to learn.

As you may know time stops for no one, and if I allow myself to focus on the negative I might miss out on some really amazing things that life has to offer. I know for sure that I can't go back to the past, I can only take the lessons that I have learned and the experiences that I have gained from it and move on. It is because of the heartaches, as well as the hardships, that in the end helped to make me to become a stronger person.

It's these things that give me the strength to continue on with my journey. I know that I can always look back on those times of my past and know that because of that one person in my life and those experiences, I am who and what I am, and try to remember the wonderful moments that I have shared with people around me.

After all these years of searching, waiting, trying, lots of patience and emotions, it seemed that my dream was coming true. I was going abroad for my first holiday, but this was going to be something different. It seemed like I had options and possibilities, and a destination with many other contradictions.

When you are young, life is full of energy and energy is always in motion — and the good news is that I would get to decide the direction. So I asked myself - which will it be? I didn't want to let myself sink slowly into the quicksand of uncertainty, doubt and fear, only to guarantee the self-fulfilling prophecy of my own failure. Or did I make the leap out of the fog and onto my upward path, eager to embrace the winding road and learn that at every step, my heart and head will be there to point me in the right direction of my dreams.

It was time I chose boldness. It was time I chose to begin.

The first step of the journey

Although it was difficult for me and everyone, it was time to make that first step of my journey.

He said 'well … we need to get you a passport'

Within days the passport was organised because as a minister and professor he knew people in high places, so that was kind of easy to organise it within days. When the passport arrived I wanted to throw a party, I was even more excited to know this would be my first travel out of the country. Also, as a bonus I would be seeing a sister that I didn't know I had.

My mind battled with my heart as to whether I would reveal to him how I felt about the whole thing and not to cause any sorrow and pain. My mind was in turmoil, but my lips remained silent. I kept telling myself that I had to maintain my composure. For a few minutes whilst waiting for him to come to the table for breakfast, I stood there by my bedroom door. This was destroying me.

That Sunday morning I designed, and rehearsed in the mirror how to create and develop conversations between us. We sat down together to have breakfast just before the church service and we both had a talk. There I had the courage to say to him.

'Although this has been difficult for me and you, I want to thank you for all your support and permitting me to go and see my sister.'

He said 'it's time for you to discover yourself even at this young age and start a relationship with your sister'

I said I was very happy that I was able to share some time with you and how I felt about the whole situation.

I had always dreamt about travelling someday and suddenly here came the trip that I had dreamed about for most of my life. This was an opportunity of a lifetime for me. Everything was arranged. He handed me a letter at the port with instructions about what to do and where to go and when and who would be meeting me when I got there.

This country that I was now visiting had a reputation of bad people who like to do Illegal stuff and I did not want to be part of those illegal immigrant people.

When I arrived there many people thought I was part of them and tried to spend time with me. I knew that could influence my mood, and I was grounded about how I spent my time, and what my perspective on the world was. One of them even tried changing my view of myself. That's why it's so important to be aware of the company I kept around me.

My sister's father was a police officer, very high up in the ranks. While waiting, a woman said to me 'there are people who you will meet in the future who will want you to do great things and they are the ones who will empower you and push you to be better.' She continued by saying 'They will inspire you to raise your standards and to believe in yourself. When you spend time with them, you leave better than you were before.'

I said to myself 'hmmm that's interesting'

A police office came and then I was taken to a hotel where I would stay for the night as my sister's father would be collecting me the following day. At this hotel there was lots of activities going on through-out the night. I couldn't sleep, because maybe I was too excited, nervous or from being disturbed by all the noise. There were police searching all the hotel rooms looking for illegal immigrants.

Living on my own without any siblings, and then going to see this family gave me time to reflect while I was at the hotel. I kept telling myself everything would be OK and I hoped that this relationship would go smoothly as this was the first time we would be meeting and seeing each other and I hoped it would be important for all of us.

I'd always had a good relationship with everyone around me, and I was looking forward to maintaining and having a good relationship with this family.

While staying inside my room at the hotel, there were so many things going around in my head. I felt I was in isolation all this time, and everyone so far was keeping this as a secret, especially my mother.

Later that evening, the whole hotel was filled with police, they were everywhere. I knew that I was OK, I wasn't afraid because I knew I was good. Everyone else was terrified, they began to panic and started to look a bit strange. Then a guy I was speaking with earlier that was staying there came up to me while I was standing on the balcony watching what was going on.

So many things were happening I got lost in the conversation he was having with me. The change of the atmosphere I was experiencing started from just one very small event in time, and one person. I could truly say my entire experience of this journey started right from this hotel.

He said, 'sorry would you do me a favour?' His voice sounded even stranger than his face.

'Depends,' I said

He said 'can I just hide in your room, just for moment please, pretty please.'

'The room is open' I said

A police officer came to me and said 'can I see your passport?'

I said 'it's in my room – let me go and get it'

He then followed me to my room. And I showed him my passport then he left and I pulled the room door shut behind me. I knew that guy was somewhere in my room but I could not see him when I was in there. He was quiet as a mouse.

There were so many challenges involved, but what was really rewarding at the end of that experience was one moment, a singular moment, when I could help someone in their time of need by which I did what I could. I felt in that moment not only that I could help but maybe I had changed this guy's life for the better. The fact that my senses told me what to do at that present moment could have brought this guy's family peace of mind. Just that one moment made me feel like the entire experience was very rewarding.

Most of the time, expectations have to be considered as a complex path to the future involving several people who we may not know and not just our will to help others. That is why it is so difficult sometimes to bet (yes, it is definitely a bet) on other people, because we can change ideas, we meet new people and discover new things. On the other hand, we may not learn anything and strongly want to stare at the same tiny point without a move or without progress.

Expectations are a straight route that we build in order to create our future while living in the present, forgetting that we do not know what is going to happen.

That guy was very desperate, as he had a family in another country who were struggling and all he wanted was to do his best to look after his family. So I didn't blame him for what had just happened or what he was doing. I knew what the situation was, I had just come from there so I didn't question him.

That evening I learnt that the right approach is to move from blame to the analysis, not why but how? Consider what went wrong and what was different. This is an interesting way of me moving myself from a guilty state of mind into a discovery state of mind, exploring the causes not as a court but as a human being, and accepting real life instead of living for the expectations.

Sometimes, this complete sense of the past, the present, and the future, makes it almost impossible to be surprised or not to expect something, which is the only disadvantage of this state of mind. In the end, this kind of mood could really transform how I was willing to act and fight for my future. I knew that I could be free of the fear of failure because I was willing to accept the consequence of the unexpected routes.

The following morning, my sister's father came and collected me from the hotel in a police car, and we started to make the journey. Everyone at the hotel saw me leave and I'm sure, started to wonder if I was also in trouble as well.

I am not a laid back person. I never have been I think. I worry and get stressed and can be quite negative sometimes. It took a long time to notice it but I lost control of how stressed I was getting before he arrived. I would randomly start a conversation in the car on the way during this long journey ahead (four hours). I struggled to relax and be still because I was feeling a bit terrified because I didn't know what to expect when I got there. I felt like I was losing my mind – thoughts were racing constantly and I kept seeing images in my head of what the place looked like or what she, my little sister would be like.

That morning the air in the mountains in that region felt very cold. The air there was still clean and fresh because it had not been mixed with pollution. The mist and fog still covered the green leaves. The sound of birds singing their bird song was very beautiful. In the mountains there were many paddy fields. Rice fields which were planted with rice that had now been yellowed and almost harvested. In addition to rice fields, there were also many gardens that were planted with tea and tobacco. At the side of the road, many trees were planted, like palm trees, which serve as water absorption during the rainy season.

Encouraged from looking at how beautiful the scenery was by looking out the window, I thought of different techniques and ways in which to cope with what was happening to me. I had learnt about mindfulness, breathing techniques, visualisation and the power of just accepting that you're experiencing anxiety and that's okay – it's going to go away eventually. It was really helpful.

When we arrived in the city it was raining cats and dogs and then we made a stop at his office in the police station. It was raining so heavy we hung back in the car hoping the rain would break, but it didn't.

This was a country with a different language (Dutch) so I said to myself wow … … 'How will I manage and get around independently through a place when I don't even know the language?'

I had these concerns as well before I started travelling to this country. I pictured walking up to every street vendor, kiosk at the shops, and taxi drivers with no ability to communicate. My travels could wind up in a storm of confusion and I'd be left feeling frustrated and lost. While that did happen from time to time, it was rare, and much less stressful than I initially expected, because there were lots of people who could speak English.

While sitting at the police station waiting for him, I started to think to myself there is so much taking place here. But hey it's a police station what should I expect. So I said to myself, if I walk up to a food stand or sit in a restaurant, it's clear I want to eat, and if I walk into a bus station, I probably want to go somewhere. Right!

Many of these practical problems would arise from not knowing the language of this country. If I had to go to the grocery, shop it may take twice as long. I may end up with a random haircut since I couldn't explain what I wanted. But I kept reminding myself that they will rarely incur long-term consequences and can usually be sorted out with a bit of extra time. In many ways, these little challenges would make this journey a bit more exciting and I could learn many great lessons in solving these problems.

When I arrived at the police station, everyone in his department was looking at me with a strange face. So I thought maybe this is how these people in this country look, or maybe because it is a police station. While I was waiting for him to finish what he was doing, this young lady came to me and said 'welcome to the honey pot.' I didn't have a clue what it meant, all I did was smile and pretend I knew what she was talking about. All that was going through my head at the time was how do I understand the language, what strategies did I have to put in place for me to get around this strange country and which techniques did I have to use to get by.

We arrived at the home where my little sister was standing on the balcony. I saw her in the distance as we made our way to the house. For some reason all I was thinking was the moment I was 'meeting my sister' was the legit scariest thing I had to do as a young human. But I said to myself it really doesn't have to be. So many questions were going through my head such as 'will she like me?' 'Will she accept me as her brother?' I kept saying to myself 'the most important thing is to just be myself.' Plus, once the first meeting was out of the way, it only gets easier. I was trying so hard to relax, but obviously I was super nervous.

The introduction was made by her father, we hugged and we kissed and her father was our translator as she only understood a little bit of English and of course I did not understand one single word of Dutch. I was asked by her father to talk a bit more about my experience of not knowing that I had a sibling sister. All I had to say was 'I didn't know.' One thing that I knew that we both had in common was the feeling that there were always situations where we both do not understand what is going on or words we both did not understand. I used to hear people often complaining of frustration that they don't understand, now I understood what they meant.

I was also introduced to a young man. I was told that he was her adopted brother who was also living there.

Even when I was sitting there, I could hear my name being called, and did not know what was being said of me. I never felt this way. As I struggled to understand and express myself, often the language was just flying by me and I did not understand most of it. This never bothered me. There were many times and situations with this language when I had trouble following the conversation but it didn't matter. I did my best to participate to the extent I could, and felt happy that I was able to do so.

The more familiar I got with certain context in this language, the better I started to communicate. I started off by learning to talk about my life and a little bit of about sports or politics. Yet for a long time could not understand television dramas.

I have learnt to recognise that even when I was having difficulty understanding, just hanging in there and listening was helping to train my mind to some extent. And to improve in a certain context I would need to expose myself to it.

The time was approaching when my little sister was going to celebrate her tenth birthday, and the family was in preparation for this big party.

In this country and culture, people celebrated their birthdays every five years. When it came to celebrations, they would feed the whole country. That's what I called a massive celebration with lots of food, dancing and flowers.

As the days went on, more and more of the family came to the house to see this brother they heard about. It was like love at first sight. Some of them spoke good English and some a mixture of

English and Dutch. I had to remember that these people are strangers to me and were not my family but some of them made me feel like family.

One thing was for sure, I had to learn their culture very quickly because things here were quite different from what I was used to. As a result, there was a time of premium on intellectual curiosity and learnability, the desire and ability to quickly grow and adapt to their culture and language and how they did things was growing very fast on me. What I knew was less relevant than what I had to learn, and knowing the answer to questions was less critical than having the ability to ask the right questions in the first place.

It was impossible to trigger deliberate changes in my culture from where I was from, but I had to actually put in place formal reward systems to entice them — and even then there was no guarantee I was going to achieve all the changes in this culture. Sadly, even when I didn't understand the importance of learning everything in this culture and language — at least in theory — I was interested in learning everything I needed to know to boost my understanding and to maximise my performance in what I was doing.

There is where I had learnt that curiosity is not just about praising and promoting myself just to display an effort to learn and develop; it's also about creating a climate that nurtures my critical thinking.

CHAPTER FIVE

Building on a learning experience

As a teenager and having the appetite to learn, I was willing to fit in with this family. Rather than trying to teach everyone everything that I knew of my culture and where I was from, very quickly I realised it wouldn't work. I started to cultivate this new environment in which I created this headspace to learn, even at this teenager age I was experiencing something new. I had decided at this point that this would be a new experience for me and 'the world won't stop for me.' Be prepared for failure - and learn from it.

As a child growing up I was learning from my experiences and the strongest way of learning what was safe and what wasn't was often driven more from painful events rather than any warnings my adopted mother and the minister had given me. While I would like to think that I've become much more intelligent and logical over time, as I got into adulthood I have also tended to learn in the same way. I was also willing to admit failures of my own, and demonstrate how the learning from any failure can be used.

It was also important to realise that failure is just part of the normal course of operation for my life, and yet something which could be monitored, proactively minimised, and learned from. Most crucially, I needed to create an environment where failure was not instantly punishable. Learning from one's mistakes was important, but this had to be done by me.

As hard as it can be to accept it, I started to believe that change was my best teacher. This had an enormous, disruptive impact in nearly all aspects of my life. New family, new environment, new country, new language. While the prospect of change on this scale was daunting, it was an opportunity to change myself for the better. In my life at this point, I started to look to embrace the change, and in doing so expanded my judgement-base, my human interaction-dependent and creative components of what was going on around me. The world was speeding up, and it certainly didn't stop for me.

First, I needed to get comfortable with all that was going on and remember myself that not everything was about the bottom line all the time. It was a tough message I had to learn very quickly – particularly in uncertain times, when some things such as understanding what was going on and the meaning behind this new culture were all liable to be deprioritised.

Secondly, I needed to get comfortable with being surrounded by this new family who thought they were better than me and they thought I didn't know anything. I knew coming to this family and to this country was a risk, but hey what did I know? I was trying my hardest to demonstrate to these people that I was willing to make a commitment by investing my time and energy so I could fit in and show the most effective way of learning everything I needed to know.

Creating the right learning environment

Being in this new environment I decided to take the initiative to learn new skills for myself; for example learning a new language and I was happy enough to make enough time to do it. Also, I wanted to show this family I was serious enough to do whatever it took to fit in.

Maybe it would give them something to talk about and I needed to understand quickly what they were saying about me.

By creating an immersive environment that stimulates my true learning I had to learn to accept "failure" as part of the learning process. Instead of me sitting worrying about things and myself, I used the time wisely by gamifying the learning process and creating simulations designed to change my behaviour and empower change, through meeting new friends outside of the family setting. I started to find things to do by meeting up with friends for a game of tennis and other sports. By having these skills in sport, it made me recognise that I could show my genuine activity and willingness to buy into becoming a part of the solution.

Another thing which fed into my learning culture was my system of how I had to create a working team with the family. I wasn't scared of getting it wrong and that meant I was more likely to try out new ideas and learn from myself and other's mistakes. No idea was too weird for me – and I wanted everyone to be part of the conversation that was beginning to start.

It was important for me at first to identify a clear sense of purpose beyond this visit. There was also an important role for me to play in creating and learning this new culture. Put simply: I wanted to see the change I had adopted within this family and the environment, and I needed to first start exhibiting the mind-set and behaviours I wanted to see from the people around me.

Whether I knew it or not, this new environment and this new family had a new learning culture that I needed to know and learn about. I knew for a fact I was biologically wired to learn new things. I couldn't help or stop myself from this learning process. Learning was necessary for my survival. It was a natural instinct. I constantly started to absorb all the information, determine what was important to me, and then decided how to act on it. The learning experiences started to happen all around me. I was allowing all of this to happen on my own.

I was also learning that I had the power to be an influence to others, whether this family were trustworthy or not. The risk taking was rewarding, even if there was harassment that had to be tolerated.

The transformative learning was starting to expand my consciousness through the conversion of other people's view of me and my capabilities. It started to act to change how I saw myself and did things by maximising my potential of where I was at this point and by making the most of the potential of all the people around me.

The visa I had was only for forty days in the country, but as the days went by I started to get very comfortable with the life in that country and in the home. The relationship with everyone started to become a bit better and people started to like me.

I had a moments of resistance and lack of trust about what I should do and whether I wanted to go back or stay many times. At any given moment, there was a compassionate, frictionless flow of people who wanted to help me to understand the culture and how things worked, but I had to allow it to happen. Deep down I believed that if anyone saw how I really was and how I felt, they would have rejected me, so I held on tightly to the mask I created. Without realising it, many of these people in this family found a way to keep their own natural peace and control was certainly one means of doing so.

Looking from the outside, one of the things I saw was what was happening to me at that very moment, where I was in this new family and how they worked and did things. But my rushing and pushing past the present moment caused me to miss out on the learning process. In my efforts to do more and get wherever I wanted to go faster, I forgot that I simply couldn't rush the process and still expect to be really successful at anything I wanted to do.

I knew and learnt very quickly that true growth was not cheap. It came with a price. My emotional maturity and seasoning came through an intimate understanding of the process of life, the love I felt within the family circle and the depth of subtleness that was achieved through a commitment of patience.

What was I looking for? What was missing in my life at this point? Maybe it was something that I saw other people and families were having and I was missing out.

Finding this circle of love was a profound experience for me and it was well worth working toward. It's what I was yearning for in my soul. A bit of fun, joy, intimacy and creativity were some of the results of the circle of love I started to experience. So, I asked myself what could I do to create more circles of love in my life? By adapting and understanding, the circle of love began to occur when my sister and I were together with completely open hearts of sharing - open with our true selves and with each other. When we are deeply connected with our core self and with the love, and we are sharing ourselves and love with others and they are doing the same, the circle of love occurs.

I knew that most people in relationships with their siblings rarely, if ever, experience such a circle of love I wanted to experience. This was because when your intent is to protect against your painful feelings rather than to learn about loving yourself and others, your heart is closed - closed to yourself, and closed to others.

Her father came to me and said he was liking the way things were with my sister and he would love it to stay that way.

CHAPTER SIX

Psychological challenges

There were no females in this house, only my sister who was now ten years of age. So it was vital that her father played the unique role of mother and father in the house for both of our childhood development. However, I realised that it had also demonstrated the negative psychological, educational, and social effects on us both as we were children who had been deprived of growing up in a home with both biological parents or parents who were married to each other.

Well as for me, I had no family of my own, I had always been around people who played the role of mother and father who were not biological. So I was getting used to it.

But as time went by or as I got older, I started to realise that my experience would suggest that growing up without a mother more extensively than fatherlessness, could cause greater damage to a child because the role of the mother is so crucial in establishing a child's ability to trust and to feel safe in relationships. I realised this when my adopted mother went away to her family because of her ill health.

Yes I knew that my sister's father also brought an array of distinctive talents to the parenting enterprise in this household as there was no wife or woman in the house. He did not even have a girlfriend. He excelled when it came to providing discipline, play and challenging both of us and not one child any more than the other. He had to embrace life's challenges. His presence in the home protected us from fear and strengthened our ability to feel safe especially as he was a police officer who carried a gun.

In the home, it wasn't just myself and my sister, there was also a young man a few years older than me and he was the step-brother of my sister. While came as a surprise, of course I saw him as my older brother.

I didn't see it as step-brother or sister or even step-father because everyone showed affection towards each other. There were no conflicted loyalties, feeling competitive with each other, or feeling pressured to have a relationship with one another. Yes there were a few unique issues of our own, such as decisions around the house and planning. His father-like attitude to all of us provided that essential role model for all of us. I loved that I had the opportunity to share the home with others as a family.

On the whole, our relationship was uncommonly open and supportive; we all strived to encourage one another to explore, and even playfully push the limits to get to know each other better.

One night I went to bed a bit early. After a few hours of sleep, I woke up in the early hours of the morning and just couldn't fall back to sleep. While lying on the bed I heard strange noises happening like knocks and footsteps coming from nowhere. As the house had a wooden floor, it was a strange experience. I laid there thinking to myself, what is going on in this house. I felt within myself that evil spirits lived in the house with this family.

I got up quietly and had a look. I looked to the left and then to the right. I saw my sister's father entering my step-brother's bedroom. I was thinking to myself why would he go into his room at this time of the night. What on earth is going on?

Later that night I heard some noise coming from that room, it was not normal noise, it was sexual noises. Unfortunately, these noises were happening too often and they continued thereafter.

The next morning, things had started to move in an uncomfortable direction for me. I kept quiet and carried on as normal, as if nothing had happened and I hadn't noticed or heard anything. My sister's father was very close with my step brother. I had never to this point noticed this before or anyone giving any sign or talking openly about sex and sexuality.

I was kind of horrified and was not feeling comfortable with what was going on in this house and I knew for sure I was not willing to be supportive with that kind of behaviour.

So many questions came into my head. 'Do the rest of the family know about this? Does my sister know about this?' Well … I suppose she was still young and maybe didn't have a clue what was going on.

In principle I didn't have a problem with what they did, but this was not for me.

My ambivalence was concerning. This became an "uncomfortable direction" for me, and I was not happy to play along or get myself involved. I was feeling very uncomfortable, perhaps because I didn't know who to talk to or who already knew, or what to say, as I had never in my life to this point experienced such things. I was trying so hard not to show how uncomfortable I was feeling about this, particularly when it was involving two men having sex.

I wanted to talk to someone. I was in total disbelief. 'This is impossible' I protested. I kept telling myself of course this wasn't really true. But it had continued for a long time, well … when I was still living there.

Many people had grown up without hearing the words "gay" or "lesbian" in those days. Therefore, I wasn't sure how to respond when someone asked me what that meant and I didn't know how to explain it to someone. It was better for me to try not to answer or ask anything or just to respond with silence or evade the question. I had to figure out how I was feeling and what I was comfortable saying or asking.

I really thought that love and relationships came from a man and a woman. I just couldn't get my head around the fact that people love each other in different ways, especially when it came to a man and man. I had learnt very quickly at this tender age that some women loved and wanted to be partners with a man and some men loved and want to be partners with a man.

I knew I had to respect them and people deserve respect. But how could I see both of them differently and how would I continue to show that respect to both of them?

Yes people can fall in love and want to be in a relationship with people of the opposite sex (this is what I knew then) but it was very strange to find out that it could happen with people of the same gender. I found it at the time a great insult and thought it was not OK. I had a serious problem with it and I became very judgemental towards couples of the same sex.

I had also learnt that sexual feelings are an important part of many people's lives and can bring a lot of pleasure. Although these feelings are exciting, they can also be complicated and confusing. At my age I did not know what they meant by being gay or homosexual. I had never heard of it. Maybe it was around but I didn't notice it. This was my first experience of two men sleeping together, but I never knew they were. They did not show in any way that they were gay, I had always seen them both as straight men. No one told me or taught me about this kind of lifestyle and neither of them came forward to share with me anything about their sexuality.

They both had protected their identities very well. Especially my sister's father, as he was very high up in the rank of the police force. I had to get my head around this situation living in this house and try to come to terms with these two men and their sexuality.

I had come to realise that two people had affected the whole of my life. One is the change from being a person who believed in one thing like there is a man and a woman and not a man and a man having sex. The other is the transformation in my awareness of what it meant to be spiritual and a Christian.

As I got older and was still living there, I had to live through the drama of seeing and maybe sometimes hearing what was going on behind closed doors. As time went by, I started to educate myself and saw a transformation of the status of lesbian, gay, bisexual and transgender people in society and a transformation of how the world was changing but I still had a lot to learn.

Yes I first had full-on sex with woman far older than me. I was young and just about a teenager and that was an experience - aside from the usual horrifying awkwardness and somewhat spontaneity of the occasion—was completely and utterly unremarkable aside from one thing: this woman wanted to have sex and she used me as her sex puppet.

I wondered to myself did anyone else know about them? Are they both a secret gay? My sister's father had not come out as openly gay. Of course, I believed that no one knew. No one other than him, and perhaps his mother (my sister's grandmother), or maybe his closest friends and some of the family. In the time that I found out about it, for days, months and years I kept it to myself but there were times when people would look at me funny. Maybe now I started to know why.

One evening I was washing the dishes, and my sister's father came to me and we were talking about what I wanted to do with my future while I was there. He had his hands on my shoulder and I said to him 'I don't like to be touched – we can talk but I hate people touching me'. I made it clear I was not interested in his or anyone's lifestyle and I would decide what I wanted to do and get back to him. After a few minutes we spoke about having a girlfriend.

He asked 'have you found a girlfriend yet?'

I said 'No, not yet'

He said 'be very careful with these Dutch girls'

I said 'don't worry, I believe I can handle it'

I continued to say to him 'I always had a genuine belief a man is a gift to women, and I was so sure with myself that there wasn't room for another person in any other sort of relationship'.

Basically I was telling him in the nicest way possible 'I was not interested in him or any gay person, and that everyone has their own preferences and no one should doubt themselves.'

I said 'my charm, my appeal and the way I view myself is enough and not everyone can have that.'

Finding a Focus

I needed a focus and a distraction as I was finding it difficult to process what I was going through, so I decided to shift my attention onto something else for a while. This was where I wanted to take a break and immerse myself in a soothing or relaxing activity that I could enjoy.

Maybe I was thinking of games in sports which would involve problem solving. It might help me to focus on solving something unrelated to what I was going through at the time. I was looking for something that can help to immerse myself in a creative or practical activity.

This situation was leading to certain thoughts and memories that were causing me to feel sad and anxious and I was looking for an outlet to distract myself from these thoughts. So I decided to find something as a distraction that would help me get my mind off upsetting or negative thoughts.

What I was most confused about was whether my sister's father liked women, because I saw how he was around women, but wasn't too sure what sort of person he was. I said to myself maybe he was finding his sexuality a bit complicated. He was attracted to woman and identified himself as straight, but also sometimes has sex with men. Aww well ... his sexuality was personal to him and that was none of my business, either way right or wrong. That's the way he feels.

This whole drama was becoming a distressing thing that I did not want to think about. Sometimes I sat and watched television and these thoughts were making me feel like I had a serious condition such as anxiety, depression, or post-traumatic stress. I did not know where to go and who to talk to. There was no such thing as a mental health professional. Not that I knew about anyway! So I had to deal with this in my own way as I knew best.

I became close friends with the neighbours opposite. So one day I went over just to clear my head and I wanted to chill out and move away from the house for a bit. They were a lovely family: mother and father with three kids: two boys and a girl. All of them were nearly the same age as me so we had something to talk about. As soon as I arrived over at the neighbour, they were so happy to see me 'We are your neighbours,' the older brother said.

I did not know if I should have jumped with joy or hugged him like my life's wish had finally come true, but still I had to show some emotion. So I laughed out loud.

He looked at me strangely. 'You okay?' he asked, 'you seem a bit worried. Come on in we are your neighbours.'

These people were living there for a while, so my sister's family and them were very close friends, but the prospect of them being in such close vicinity that they could see me trot about in my crumpled home-wear, with my unkempt hair and worn out footwear as I went to the grocery store or walked over to the neighbourhood cafeteria had me a bit apprehensive.

My sister moved to live with her grandmother, as they found a better school there. So during the week (Monday to Friday) she would be there and on the weekend she would return back to her father. So most of the days in the week I was home alone, as my step-brother was working and of course my sister's father would be at work. So I became lonely and bored.

Most evenings I would go over and chill out with my neighbours. We all got along well, had some great laughs and we all enjoyed ourselves. One evening I went over and only the sister was there. So I stayed and we had a good chat, we spoke about various different pop songs in different languages (English and Dutch). She had a walkman cassette player, and we were playing different songs and we were sharing the headphones, then one of the songs took our fancy.

She said 'people normally drink alcohol to enjoy this song'. We had played so many songs, the battery died. She said, she had an electrical connection for the player in her room so we should go to the bedroom and continue to play and listen to the songs.

She went out of the room and came back with two plastic cups and two small bottles. One was a homemade drink and the other was alcohol. I can remember, although I'd had some drinks, sitting in her room on that single bed with the mattress overly springy and a coarse plastic coating, attempting to be Michael Jackson dancing on the bed.

That was the first time I ever had alcohol, so it went straight to my head and we both were on top of the world as the music continued to play in our shared head-set.

She said to me 'you are very handsome'

I said to her 'you are beautiful'

Next thing I knew we were kissing each other passionately. Then my hands were all over her and she was doing the same. It was clear that both of us were intoxicated, but it was a party after all. I felt quite drunk and so was she.

How did things develop so quickly from us being together in the front/living room, then to the bedroom, to us having slightly unsuccessful sex?

All I know is that one moment we were listening, dancing, talking, and the next minute, well … we weren't. I didn't tell her that I'd had sex with someone before; instead, saturated with the alcohol and inflated by nerves, I was swept up in the emotion.

We were both teenagers, she wanted to experiment, and I was precocious and restless. I was a lonely child at the house and she was alone and needed company. I took the advancement of my early sexual experiences into my own hands and I did what we all do. I had thrilling, and now looking back, precarious hook ups with her, going far but never all the way. I know now that we both could define exactly what constitutes sex for ourselves, but when we were both young, the only sex education came in the shape of looking at the magazines and trying and experimenting for yourself.

After a few months we decided to go all the way. I was her first but I knew that from the start. We ended up having sex secretly without anyone knowing. She would come over to mine and I would go over to hers when everyone was gone.

After a year or so, we had to move to another house, as my sister's father was moved to another police station and that station came with a house. The journey was two and half hours' drive away and we both did not have our driving licence or know how to drive. There were no cell or mobile phones so all we had was a house phone. We spoke every day for about five weeks after we moved. Then the house phone was not working as they were changing and upgrading the line, so we couldn't make contact for a while.

When the line was up and running, I phoned her and she was not home. Well … that's what her brother told me at the time. She continued to refuse to speak to me even though I kept trying and trying. I was thinking what did I do wrong? Why was she so upset with me? Why was she not talking with me? Until this day I did not get an answer.

'So here we go again' I said to myself

I found that there are many aspects of loving someone not only sexuality, but falling deeply in love and I really thought I had it all matched up or that I understood the difference. However, I was still questioning myself 'am I good lover or a good partner?' or 'is everyone I am meeting with, just seeing me as a sex object?' Everyone kept saying 'you are so handsome' but later disappeared.

Intimacy and physical touch

As I grew into my late-teens, I found myself a job. I was so happy to have found this job but the only problem was that I was the only male working there among seven women. All of them were a bit older or far older than me.

At first it was Ok, working there. I got to know more of each one of them. I noticed every morning they kept moving me from one side of the room to another.

Do you ever feel really weird sometimes and you can't explain it?

Well for me it was a really unsettling feeling. The world around me didn't seem real and I just felt really disconnected. It was like I wanted to be happy but I just didn't feel normal and nothing around me seemed real.

I felt a bit of anxiety, but it felt imperceptible because it was so hard to pin down. But when I was feeling like something was not quite right, there was a pretty good chance it was anxiety. I was experiencing a feeling of uneasiness and a physical sensation I couldn't quite place. It felt like symptoms of anxiety rearing its head.

It was a strange feeling when someone asked 'what's wrong' and my honest response was 'I just don't feel right.' Sometimes I could easily articulate my emotional state - sad, mad, stressed or ticked off. Other times, I just felt weird.

Sometimes those weird feelings passed quickly and sometimes I would relate it to specific situations I was going through. Other times, that odd feeling would just hang around. When that happened, I thought it would be smart and proactive to try and talk to someone about how I was feeling. I hoped it would make me feel better faster. There were many times I felt slightly or subtly off. My body was naturally responding to fear. But I didn't say anything to anyone. I just carried on as normal.

One morning I went to work as normal, saying 'Hi' to everyone, we started talking about any and everything. Who did what and who went where. Everything was going fine that day. During my lunch break I would take a walk up the road, just to be away from all these women. On my return I could smell this strong perfume. But I did not say anything. Why should I because hey there are women in here.

The boss who was a woman called me into her office and said that she would like me to do her a favour. She asked if I could take her husband's motorbike and deliver some of these products to a customer because her husband was not feeling well. I had never ridden a motorbike in my life, but I was happy to give it a go. I went outside and looked at the bike. It looked straight forward, so I test rode it and everything was OK and ready for the delivery.

The ladies prepared the packages nicely for me and I took the packages, secured them carefully at the back of the bike and off I went to get them delivered.

I got a bit lost on the way because I did not know where I was going so I got there a bit late and the customer was waiting for me. There were no such thing as maps, or a Sat NAV. All I needed to do was to get to the area and keep asking everyone for directions until I found the place.

I came back to the work place very late to return the bike and everyone had gone. Well ... so I thought. Everywhere seem locked and no one was around.

As soon as I parked the bike in a safe place, I heard a knocking coming from the window. When I looked up there was one of the women standing there, trying to say something to me, but I couldn't hear her properly so I went closer to the window.

She said 'I am locked in'

'How did that happen?' I replied

She said 'I was in the toilet and when I came out everyone was gone and they locked the door.'

I was thinking 'this is not good'

I was trying to think of a solution for this problem. I saw a window that was big enough for me to get through because of my slimness, so I took the bike around to where the window was and I stood on it and managed to get through the window.

When I got inside, I could smell this strong perfume but again I did not say anything. I was only thinking of getting her out of this building so we both can go home. While standing there right next to her, she held my hands and said 'what are we going to do?' Not even thinking straight I said 'we will have to work something out.' She was far bigger than me (in size) and also older.

As I was trying to work this problem out I walked towards the main door and I looked to my left and saw a piece of cloth on the chair. I went and picked it up and was about to put it in the bin. I then realised that it was a woman's underwear that was on the chair (panties). She saw me pick it up and said 'sorry that's mine. I am not wearing any at the moment.'

I said "OK"

She took it from me and said 'would you like to put it back on for me?'

I stood there in silence not knowing what to do or say.

Then I sat down on the chair, thinking to myself what is going on here, and what is this woman up to. Sweat started to pour down my face. I'm not even sure if that was because it was hot or because I was nervous or in shock?

The next think I remember, she sat on me facing towards me without any panties on and she was undoing my pants. When she was finished with that she undid her top and put her breast into my mouth. No was around and the place was dead quiet but she was making so much noise I did not know what was going on.

This woman was about ten years older than me. She whispered in my ear 'I wanted you for so long. I was giving you all the signs so I have to take it.'

The choices I made in these places of work with females as working mates involved several factors especially the age differences, their appearance, the kind of intelligence they had over me, and their funny sense of humour.

She continued enjoying herself on top of me and said 'this is your welcome gift.' I just sat there not knowing what to do and my little mini me was hard as ever. She said 'I will show you all about lovemaking, because you are still a virgin.'

'Men lust and we women want to feel desired'. She said

'I will show you, come on - I want to follow your lead and I will come during the intercourse.' She said to me.

When everything was all done she said to me 'I am very happy with our level of sexual activity. I am very satisfied, and I would like to have sex more often with you'

Looking back now it seemed at the time I believed she had outgrown the need for safer sex and she was using me as a practice tool. This woman had no hesitancy about broaching the topic of sexual practices with me and I thought maybe her partner was reluctant to have sex with her.

She wanted to continue her sex life longer and improve the opportunities she did not have with young men like myself. I wasn't too sure if she was a widow, divorced, or otherwise single for her to pounce on me and to enter into a sexual relationship with me. After all was said and done, this woman had the keys all along in her bag. Then she said to me with a big smile 'Take me home on that bike.'

This was an experience I will never forget as long as I live. But I must say I have learnt so much in that little time of enjoyment. Mostly for her.

What I have learnt in this experience is that sex can be a powerful emotional experience and a great tool for protecting or improving health because I felt so damn good afterwards. Also, it's certainly not only for the young. The need for intimacy was ageless and no matter what your gender.

It seemed for her she was longing for it for a long time, and I came along at the right time for her. She felt wiser and bolder to attack me in this way and knew what worked best for her when it came to her sex life. She had a great deal more self-confidence and self-awareness than me and I felt released from the unrealistic ideals of my youth and prejudices of others. She was seeking to restart or improve her sex life and was also ready to try new things which was a learning experience for me as well.

From there on then, I had an open-mind for women. I continued to work there because I needed the money but seeing her everyday became a distraction. She got promoted in the job, and she became very demanding about who I should be talking to and where I should be sitting.

Yes, we continued to do it a few more times with her demands and I did whatever she said to keep my job and to make her happy. That made my experience and my sex life more exciting. I have learnt strategies to improve my communication skills such as using humour, being gentle and how to tease just to make sex more pleasurable.

My working hours were from Monday to Friday. One day in the week my boss called me into the office and said, she would like me to work on Saturday because a lot of deliveries needed to get to the customers before Monday. It was extra money so why not? I arrived at the time she told me. When I got there, she was sitting on the table in her office and said she already got someone else to do the delivery. I was a bit upset because I was looking forward to the extra money to go clubbing later that evening. Then she said don't worry because I was there she was going to pay me for the day, so I didn't feel as if she had wasted my time. When I stepped into her office, she told me not to worry and she would make it up to me for coming all this way. It would be worth my while.

She asked me to close the door behind me.

She said 'I have to ask you something'

I started to get a bit nervous, wondering what had I done wrong.

She said 'I came into the office and the office had a funny smell. Do you know anything about that?'

Of course I said 'No', because seriously I did not have a clue what she was talking about.

She got off the table and walked closely towards me and pushed me towards the closed door and said 'are you sure?'

I said 'No, I don't know what you are talking about.'

She said to me 'the more you talk, the more you're tickling my mood'

I was thinking what was this woman talking about?

She then said to me 'have no fear – just give me what I desire.'

So I said 'and what is that?'

'Don't you find me attractive, because I find you very handsome and attractive' she said, talking extra close to my face.

The next thing I knew we were kissing. Hands were all over the place on each other's body. This woman could have been my mother. She said 'please don't stop me. I want to try something new. I want to take pleasure in enjoying this.'

She was a big woman and next thing I knew my mini me was in her mouth and she was having a great time with it and then I was on top of her on her table in the office. It was wild sex. It seemed to me she had not had sex for a very long time. As a matter of fact she nearly killed me. I was so tired from it all.

Why did I feel like the most emotional person in the room?

I left there that day feeling so emotional, and I told myself this was not normal. I wanted to cry out loud, I wanted to scream. On my way home for some reason I stood away from the public eye, so no could see me and I had an outburst crying session, asking myself why me, what's wrong with me? Why am I feeling *so* emotional?

This feeling heightened my emotions and I was unable to control these emotions I was feeling. I felt like I was going through some sort of underlying health condition, such as depression or my hormones started to play up.

'Does everyone feel this way after having sex?', I asked myself. I knew I had sex before but this time was different. Sometimes I was feeling happy, next minute I was sad, low, and exhilarated. Was I human? Does everyone process this sort of event and emotions differently? All these questions were going through my head.

I went home that day, went to my room and sat there just staring at the wall. I felt so alienated. I had no one to talk to and to be honest I was afraid to speak to anyone.

These emotions were interfering with my day-to-day life. I just couldn't stay focused on what I was doing. I felt things a bit more than others, and some days I felt a bit extra sensitive.

While I was sitting on the bed, my sister's father came into the room and asked 'what's the problem?'

I said 'nothing'

He was not the one to speak to regarding my problem, especially when it came to sex.

He said to me 'you smell funny. You need a shower.'

I think he could have smelled that I had sex or sensed it.

So I went to have a shower. On the way to the bathroom, he said to me 'I can join you and we can talk about it'

I said 'no thank you, I will be fine' and I was very serious about what I had said.

After a few months I left the job, but continued to see the first woman who I used to work it. I used to go around to see her about three times a week. We were seeing each other for about six months. Every time I went to see her, all she wanted was sex all night. One day I went to see her late in the evening. Her brother said she was not home so I went away and came back the following day. I got the same message. 'She is not here.'

This went on for a whole week. One day I decided to pop round by her work place, because it was good to catch up with old friends. On my way to the place, as I turned the corner, I saw her standing at the main gate with a guy that I knew. He was also a police office and worked next to my sister's father office. I had never spoken to him so he did not know me but I think he knew who I was.

While standing there, I saw her enter into his car and they drove away with speed. Maybe they saw me. So I went back to her house and I saw his car parked outside and when I was just about to enter through the gate. I heard sexual noises coming from her room, as it was on the ground floor and the window was open.

I was so confused I turned around quickly and went on my way back home. My heart broke into a million pieces. I burst into tears and ran. I couldn't believe she would do that to me. In those days I was not driving, everything I did was on foot. I walked everywhere so it felt like the longest walk back to my house. I couldn't believe it, I could hear them and felt sick.

That weekend I needed to clear my head, so I decided to call my step-dad's brother, because he was a party boy. He was always in a night club and I wanted to go out and let off some steam, drink and get drunk.

The night club we wanted to go to is one my sister's father was afraid of me going to because of its history. I wanted to go because I wanted to be in a different environment and secondly there was a well-known band playing there and I wanted to be there.

When we arrived, the club was full of people. There were people everywhere. Good music was playing. I got my drink and went straight to the dance floor to let off some steam.

I met some new friends and we were having a great time. Then the venue manager started to crack down harder on underage drinking and it soon became increasingly difficult to go and get more alcoholic drinks. My new friends who were or looked much older than myself went and got the drinks for me.

In this nightclub there were all kind of things taking place, such as white power and the biggest roll ups you've ever seen. It was not cigarettes (coke and weed)! I felt, in my increasingly anxious and deflated state, that I was being left behind, so I joined in that party. As this was my first time going to a nightclub in this country, I was giving it all that I had. I was letting my hair down and enjoying myself, and no one was going to stop me. I found it was helping me mentally.

While I was there I came outside to get some fresh-air as it was a bit too hot and I was a bit drunk. While standing outside I saw my neighbour from where I used to live. I went to her and said 'Hello beautiful'. She gave me a big hug and we spoke about what had happened in the past. She said she was sorry for what she had done.

Feeling this horny and dealing with newly minted sexual desires was making me feel simultaneously overwhelmed, confused and excited all at the same time. In addition to my cravings and experiencing these tingles, I was more aware than usual. Fantasies were running wild through my head and I was even feeling more stressed.

While she was talking to me I just couldn't stop fantasising about her. I kept looking at her with my drunk self from her hair all the way down to her toes. I started to link it all back to her bedroom and my horniness.

She invited me back to her place so we could talk. Well I was so drunk and horny, we both took a taxi to her place and we ended up having a one-night-stand. I remembered the early days when I first met her but we never had sex. I was thinking I don't want this opportunity to pass me byand the way I was feeling I would not let this woman go this time.

Just imagine feeling tingles in places you've never felt them and wanting to kiss this woman standing in front of you. I must say that I felt empowered by having sex with her, but the whole experience left a lot to be desired. While I knew it wouldn't be like this again in a hurry, I took the opportunity because I may not see her again. I tried to stay in contact with her, but it was hard work. I was not getting hold of her or she was not answering the phone so I knew that nothing was really going to happen for the future.

I was out one day with my family, and I saw this woman in the distance walking towards me. As she was approaching me, I realised she was heavily pregnant. I could not believe my eyes. She was very shocked, embarrassed and surprised to see me. I said 'Hi' to her. I even called her name because I wanted her to know that I knew it was her. She stopped and we spoke. The first thing I remember her saying to me was 'I am very sorry. You didn't deserve the way I treated you.'

I said 'it's OK, we both have moved on.'

In returned she said 'I need to tell you that I came on to you quite strongly. I wanted to have sex so I could get pregnant. I wanted your children because of your good looks.'

This took me by surprise. It didn't even cross my mind about using protection, because I did not know anything about protection. She started talking about her body clock, and how desperate she was to have a child and she saw me as a perfect candidate. All this was over my head. She said she found someone else who got her pregnant and I had nothing to worry about and I, unfortunately, believed everything she said.

We went our separate ways that day and within a few days I received a letter from her, saying that she was looking to meet up. I wasn't interested as I'd recently gotten out of this relationship and was not willing to meet with her and her ready-made family. In the letter it said that the child's father was no longer around but I did not care. I didn't want to be hurt and I didn't want her or myself to feel used. I did not even reply to her letter. I just brushed it under the carpet and moved on as if nothing happened.

She wrote another letter and this time sent it through a friend that we both knew. She said in the letter that she really wanted to see me and it was very important but I was reluctant. I told the friend that I was completely devastated and in shock with everything and I was willing for us to remain friends. I only wanted to be friends as I did not want to lead her on and wanted nothing to do with her newly created family. Within three and a half weeks of receiving her last letter she wrote to me again and broke the news that she had a baby boy. I didn't want to discuss it anymore and I refused to speak to her. I tried on numerous occasions to avoid her. In the end I told her I wanted nothing to do with her and to never contact me again.

Every time I find myself between a rock and a hard place, contemplating whether to fight or fly or, when faced with confrontation, my mind tells me to avoid the situation at all costs. Flee it is.

I realised that there are people who seek to confront issues head-on and there are those who avoid confrontation in favour of letting the problem naturally dissipate. If I am the latter, it's neither a poor quality nor a wholly positive quality to steer clear of arguments and conflicts, as it has its fair share of benefits and consequences.

Fake

I did not want to become that person who is a counterfeit or not a genuine person or even be an imitation of another person. I wanted to be me.

Before I learnt how to make a masterpiece, I had to learn the process of making the masterpieces. The image and the creativeness of myself is one of a kind and this is the value placed on me by the creator. All of this was in God's plan.

Many times there was a question that came to the forefront of my mind, am I a masterpiece or someone else's side-piece?

The reason for this question is because of the feeling of anger and even the envy that my friends or acquaintances showed towards me because of the attention but I felt cheated. Maybe I needed that attention because I was feeling lonely. My sister was staying or even living at her grandparents and here I was again, all alone.

But what I'd also discovered through conversations with friends and acquaintances is how the offshoot of side-piece jealousy is side-piece shame, which is the feeling one gets when they decide to start dating someone else other than the person they're a side piece to.

I am very curious without being judgmental and I don't believe in belittling other people, although many so-called friends can show massive levels of raw ignorance with embarrassing behaviour.

I decided to start casually dating and hooking up with other people (females) and some I had met through friends. It certainly wasn't serious but it went on for a couple of months before fizzling out. I ran into some of them at different events and house parties and sometimes I got completely flustered as I talked to other females.

There were at times I reconsidered putting that fake smile on my face to show everyone that I was alright.

There were times when I was feeling the pressure to exude positivity in some of the circle of family and friends because in the back of my mind I was thinking that they all knew what the situation was with my sister's father, but no one was willing to come forward to ask or say anything to me. It was becoming a toxic positivity or simply taking the fake-it-until-you-make-it mentality. I started to portray my emotions everywhere I went all because everyone was getting to know who I was or who I was related to. Believe you me it was becoming very serious with implications on my life.

The outer surface of acting was what I was faking and what I was displaying to other people. Inside I was very upset and frustrated, but on the outside, I was trying my best to be pleasant and positive. The deep acting was trying to change how I felt inside. When I was deep acting, I was actually trying to align how I felt with how I was interacting with other people.

As time went on, I decided to analyse both deep and surface acting. These feelings of mine were of being a fraud or an imposter. I asked myself so many times 'does this happen everyone? Were there other people suffering in silence more than others'? I have learnt over the years that it even has a name: the "imposter phenomenon."

I felt like I was play-acting through life, earning the trust and faith I didn't deserve and picking up kudos that life handed to me by mistake.

It was the habit of my mind that was always denigrating my achievements to minimise the effort I was actually putting in. I was afraid of failure. I was still a child (by law) and so far in my childhood I had to learnt very quickly the reality of life experiences which included a lot of put-downs and criticisms, the dismissals and the being ignored. Up to this point of my life there was no praise for my intellect and there were always those that pooh-poohed it. I was prone to looking over my shoulder, seeing what everyone else was doing or saying behind my back.

Many times I described myself as being plagued by extreme self-doubt and a feeling of faking it through my teenager life. This was especially true for me who grew up without my biological parents and to me I felt I was high in narcissistic traits.

My sister had her family and I had to remind myself that these people were not my family. They were only accepting me because I was the brother of my sister, which everyone knew. On top of that, she was the first grand-child in the family, so she became the favourite and I was the outsider who was trying so hard to play favourite to fit in. In doing so, I was being used through a shaming and blaming system to bring the wayward into line, as well as being the controlling, combative, and dismissive brother, whom many were hypercritical of. That, too, contributed to feeling like an imposter.

I realised that when I was feeling like an imposter, I tended to over-prepare and work in such a way to impress other. I was trying so hard to show my perfectionism, while also procrastinating, which was bolstering their vision of myself as fraudulent.

There were times when I would make excuses for my successes and I tended to attribute my achievements to dumb luck or being in the right place at the right time. The problem with feeling like an imposter was that it robed me of the pleasure and pride in my very real achievements.

Even though I was struggling to navigate my way through this family and getting to know them, as the months and years went by, I had to work even harder to continue to show some respect. However, I kept everything inside of me just for a peaceful life for myself.

I must admit, I did not always know what to believe. I wanted to trust the people around me to tell me the truth and let me know what I had to deal with but they were all acting ethical. I learnt to bounce between sadness at my own cynicism and pride in my healthy scepticism that kept me alert and engaged.

CHAPTER SEVEN

Another signal

There were threats and signs. But I have to say that I was not particularly interested in what they were, but rather that there were precisely signs of what was to come and where I wanted to be. It was an impression that was conveying sense to me; it also had the effect of making something else came to mind.

Through my experience of things and in my observation and memory, I sometimes knew that there was some sort of fire there, even if I could only see the smoke. All of this started to demonstrate my anger, which was signifying my mood as a sad person, even without wishing it to do so.

Welcome to my wonderful world of riding bikes. Bicycles were my freedom. It provided me exercise, transportation and meditation all at once. First, I needed to actually get a bike. It only seemed daunting at first because most people in my circle were driving.

I was too young to get my driver's licence. So I decided to get myself a bicycle. I was very proud of my two-wheeler. I did look after it because I knew that was the only thing I had to get around.

I was just an average person and getting myself a new bike felt great, but it took me a couple of weeks pondering over which machine to go for. The perfect bike could be my companion for years to come until I was ready to get my driver's licence. On the other hand, going for the wrong machine could have spelt a very quick end to my love affair with cycling, and a permanent home in the shed for my new wheels.

This was getting a bit too much for me. Wondering around the place to start with there's a myriad of different styles of bikes, and they were all designed to fit my personal and certain criteria in different ways. The frames and components had to vary to cater for different road surfaces, luggage requirements, attitudes and levels of performance… as well as my wallet size.

I knew I needed to find a new job but finding the kind of work and a job that I loved was often a bit of a journey. I was in the process of learning about myself and the world of work before me in order to land on something that felt in alignment with me.

After buying the new bike I wanted, it was time to look for a job. While looking for a job, my sister's father said to me that his aunt who is the owner and director of the pharmaceutical company in the city was looking for someone to work in the administration department. I said yes, because it was different and I was so happy and looking forward to it. He set up the meeting and we went to meet her on the Friday, knowing in the back of my head, I had no idea what this job entailed and I had no experience in the pharmaceutical industry.

We arrived at this nice place. Basically it was a pharmacy with only women working there. Not one male in sight…. oh and a cat sleeping in her office. She said she was looking for a senior clinical project administrator with ideally two years' experience or equivalent. I knew I was already out even before I started.

However, because everyone knew that I didn't have any of the above, she was willing to train me. Everyone has to start somewhere right!! I was looking forward to be wearing the white overalls. The whole place smelled funny, but of course it was a pharmacy. Medicine was being made and prepared there for the patients and the doctor's surgeries were across the road.

After a few days I got to know everyone that worked there. There was a small group of six people working at the preparation section and I was mostly in the office getting all the prescriptions filed, invoicing to the different doctor's offices and also ordering the next set of medication. I was becoming good at it - people told me so all the time. It came easily to me, and it was a very comfortable career path.

Working in this environment with only women (again!) was putting me on the edge. But the good news was I was alone in an office hoping to mind my own business. Sometimes it was a bit lonely (well … sometimes the cat might come in and give me a visit) and boring. Don't get me wrong - it was *okay*. I learned a lot and worked with some great people.

I envied those folks who had a spring in their step on the way to work - people who absolutely loved what they did and couldn't wait to roll up their sleeves and get busy on the job. I wanted to be one of those people on the production floor. So what I began to do was I found myself a routine. I would get into work early and get through the paperwork quickly, finish my work and go on the production floor and offer to help.

The boss saw how keen I was in the work environment and she encouraged me to go and help when necessary so I finally went for it. It had been nearly a year working there, and while there I had many bumps along the way, I could now say with full confidence that I really started to enjoy and love what I was doing. I would go and help sometimes at the front desk, taking the prescriptions from the customers and then gave it to the production team. When they were very busy (which was most days) they would ask me to get it ready. I was getting the creams and powers and mixing it all together and getting it ready for the customers.

Sometimes I may just not be the best judge of what makes me happy. If you ask the people who know me intimately (which was not much) when I seemed to be the happiest and what I do the most enthusiastically, their answers may surprise you.

Every month there would be some students who came to the company to carry out their practical. Some of them had completed their master of pharmacy degree and some were trainees who were building up a portfolio of evidence to demonstrate their competency whilst being observed at work.

I have learnt that this high degree was offered by Schools of Pharmacy at a number of universities in the country. The course was undertaken as the first part of the route to registration for those wishing to become a pharmacist within the country. This programme integrated science and practice and equipped students with the theoretical knowledge, professional behaviours and clinical skills that were required to become a pharmacist. It was normally a four-year programme and needed to be completed successfully in order to enter the one-year of pre-registration training. That's why every month, there were two or three new faces on the production floor.

I was thinking, maybe this was something I would be interested in for the long run, as I was enjoying this, and I found a job and a career I loved. Learning while training to become a pharmacist involved understanding and demonstrating how to deliver the safe and effective patient-centred care which patients and the public expect from pharmacy professionals.

With a bit more investigation of how to get started, it was pointed out to me that I couldn't do it because I was too young and I did not have a university level the qualification and most of all I was not a citizen of that country. I then realised that for this sort of career type you needed money and knowing the right people. Reaching up to those levels was not going to be easy for me and in fact, it was not possible. So I just had to humble myself and continuing to do what I was enjoying.

Starting this job, within the first months, weeks, or even hours, I quickly realised this was just the job for me because I was loving it more and more. So I asked myself over and over again and wondered, 'Am I already for this?' My heart and soul wanted me to get more out of this and make something of myself but then some of the advice I heard and the thoughts I was having made me pause. I may have had thoughts around not wanting to look to be the bad employee or burn a bridge with my current employer. Some of the time I felt that I was 'throwing away' opportunities and not using the chance to 'leverage' this job, and that I had 'wasted' the time etc. These were just a few of the things that were running through my mind and created a lot of fear, anxiety and inner conflict.

I decided to spend a few hours on trying to develop a letter and my own application and see just how far I could get with it. I thought this would give me some confidence when I decided to implement an application as a solution somewhere in the future. I posted it to the Pharmacist Education Training Company. Let's be honest, I was not sure what was going to happen, but at least I could say I had tried.

Establish oneself

In one of the months there were a new set of young ladies who came for the practical training and I met this girl nearly my age (a few years older) who was there for her training. I then approached her and we introduced ourselves to each other, as this was a pattern I had always done for the time working there. There was something different about her compared to all the other women that came there.

I had known for years that I was extremely insecure. I *knew* I was not the best looking person growing up and I was scared to smile because I didn't know how other people would take it. I tried my best to dress properly and try and look good with my outer appearance. I had always believed my appearance was the reason no one ever showed interest in me for the long run. Maybe it was the way I dressed. I would call myself shy. I was devastatingly insecure about both my appearance and lifestyle (being a loser/loner).

Since I used to spend so much time on the production floor, it was normal and even natural to develop a working relationship with everyone. This woman was different. She came across very bold and spoke what was her mind. There was no holding back.

She said to me 'what's a handsome and good looking man like you working here with all these women'?

'I am just the administrator in the office' I replied

She continued by saying 'well ... the boss must be very lucky to have such an attractive man like you working here'

I said 'if you say so'

I knew in my head that this was only a work mate conversation. Then the next day one of her colleagues said to me she really likes you and she was flirting with you. I was just making sure I was keeping things friendly, and being careful not to let things go bad and end up in an uncomfortable working environment for both of us.

I know for sure that there's one aspect of communication that can really help set me apart from others which is my ability to listen. All I heard from her was a type of work mate banter. The manner in which she was speaking came across to me that she was getting a bit jealous which was making it relatively easy for her to say that her colleague was flirting with me.

I have learnt that being a good listener takes a lot of skill. Listening allows me to evaluate a situation from another perspective, to put myself in someone else's shoes, and understand a different point of view. It gives me time to reflect on what's being said and formulate a productive response.

At this point in my life I believed I was mastering the art of communication in all of its forms – speaking, writing, and virtual. I was learning to be confident in my ability to deliver a message face to face. Paying as much attention to the delivery of my message as well as the way in which what I was saying was received.

As she was talking I kept smiling at her. I kept it simple, and continued to be polite and kind because I think that was a great way to subtly hint that I was listening to her.

My workplace was a professional atmosphere, so livening up a bit and being friendly and outgoing could set me apart to her from the other people at work. A simple smile or a joke is an appropriate form of my communication but she was seeing it as flirting, and I didn't think I was crossing any professional lines. She kept smiling at me throughout the day, but I saw it as a form of her politeness and that's the way she was. So I kept smiling back at her, because honestly I was getting and feeling a bit shy and embarrassed not to.

I went back to my office and got some more work admin done. A couple of hours later while sitting there concentrating on what I was doing, I heard a knock on the door.

I said 'come in'

As she opened the door and stepped in she said 'of course I would like you to come'

At that time I didn't know what that meant.

She showed me a prescription from one of the doctor's for a patient and said 'can you make out what that says?'

In those day doctors' handwriting was horrible. All prescriptions were written out by hand and none of us could understand what it said. So I called the doctor and found out what the medication was he had written. I handed it back to her and while she was taking it from me, she touched my fingers and said 'you have lovely fingers.'

With my shyness I said 'thank you'

As the day went on, I started to feel a bit hungry so I decided it was time to eat and I got up and started making my way out to get something to eat. On my way out I was stopped by a patient who was waiting to be served as she desperately needed my help. The patient said that her son was very ill and she needed the medication urgently and her son was alone at home. I took the prescription, turned around and got the medication prepared for her with help from this young woman as she was the only one who wasn't that busy at the time. I explained to her that it was very urgent and asked if she could help me? She said 'of course I can help you at any time'

'Thank you' I replied

She looked at me and said 'what can you do for me in return?'

I said 'I am going for lunch and I could bring you back something if you wish'

She said 'we can go together'

I said 'OK'

We went to a restaurant nearby and we both sat down to order our food. She did not eat anything, all she did was drink a soft drink. While sitting there she said to me with a soft and quiet voice in my ear 'your shyness is cute and you should just be yourself' but I was a bit nervous, shaky and this was a bit socially awkward.

At the end of the working day, we all said goodbye to each other and I took my bike and off I went. She saw me with my bike as I came out of the front gate. She said to me 'I would love you to ride me on your bike.'

I wasn't too sure if it was a joke, but I took it and made a light-hearted joke and said 'sure you can.'

She then said 'I am serious, and I am going to hold you to that.'

I knew that we both had at least one thing in common, we were friends at work. I was trying so hard to avoid petty gossip about co-workers at work. I knew that I was a positive person, not a downer. I was always trying to avoid any inappropriate jokes at work and keeping things friendly and light.

A couple of weeks later she came to me and said that her exams were coming up. She said she had to get her assignment done and as it was a massive project so most nights she was studying late. Knowing the person I was and still am, I innocently offered to help in the best way I could. I asked her if she needed anything, or if there was anything I could do for her. I was only being a friend and helpful, but also showing her that I was interested in spending some extra time with her to help her with her studies.

Without any hesitation in her voice she said 'yes please – when?'

I said 'whenever you are ready, maybe one evening after work.'

She looked at me with strong eye contact. She gave me a hug and wouldn't let go of me and said 'I am so looking forward to it'. We both set a day.

She was super excited that I was coming over to her place. I only saw it as a friend coming over to help, and not a crush has invited me over but suddenly the nervousness hit me. Whether I was meeting the family, or just spending quality study time together, the number one rule was to be honest, courteous, and respectful.

In those days there weren't any cell or mobile phones, all we had was a land-line telephone and I didn't take her number. That day I went to work as normal but she wasn't there, which I suspected was due to the fact she had her studying to do. After work, I decided to go over to her place as that was the day we both set.

I knew that she would feel more comfortable in her own home but I was feeling a bit nervous and a bit uncomfortable going there, not knowing what she was expecting me to do. All I knew is that I was going there to be some company and help the best way I could.

She saw me coming, and when I arrived at her house I saw her coming down the stairs to meet me. It was a massive and nice house.

I looked at the house and I said to myself 'Wow, these people are rich.' Look at this house and the nice cars parked here.' This girl was 'Rich, Spoiled and Beautiful.' She came out with a tagline top and she was looking fabulous! She was wearing a royal blue stretchy cotton top with feminine styling and fit. She had a head full of gorgeous dark hair styled into a vintage hairstyle and she was winking, full of confidence and very flirty when she came out to meet me. She came out with a bright smile and she give me a big hug. I felt that her top was super soft, long, stretchy and fitted.

These people were living large. Her father had owned some kind of company. They even had their own plane. People were talking about debt and having to work two jobs and these people had it all. I could not believe that there were people living like this. In my head I was thinking 'what kind of life is this?'

She said 'put your bike in the shed as there are lots of thieves in this area'.

She walked with me to the shed. I parked and locked my bike, then she came in behind me with a towel in her hands and said 'it's so hot today and you are sweating. Use this and wipe yourself.'

When she was handing me the towel, she said 'let me help you.'

It was very hot on that day, but there was a nice breeze and I started to feel a chill and cold as she was wiping my face. She got a bit closer to me and the next thing I knew, she was kissing me on the lips and pushing me in the corner while she was shutting the door.

Being alone with this woman felt a bit scary at first and having the interaction play out in this shed I was becoming less at ease. As she already had her agenda set out, there was no need appealing with her to stop so I went along with it, but in my head I was thinking 'here we go again'!

She did dress nicely and appropriately for the occasion. I was trying to put up a bit of a façade but she wasn't having it. The next thing I knew and remember was my pants were already down, followed by her underwear coming off. She took my hands and let me know that this was serious and she whispered to me 'I am fresh and ready for you. I need it now'!

It was so easy to let my guard down and show the real me. There was no way I was going to stop her and she made that clear in her actions.

When it was all over, she said 'meet me upstairs.'

She took her things quickly and she left me in the shed and I was thinking what just happened, and where has she gone.

As I was walking towards the steps I saw a gentleman coming towards me from his car. Feeling a bit awkward and unsure what to do, I said hello to him and he asked who I was. I told him I was here to help my colleague with her studies. He said he was her father. I was thinking oh my gosh, that was close.

When I got into the house she was sitting there with all her books ready for her study. As I entered the house my eyes were all over the place looking at the decorations, old pictures, music and book collections. These were all excellent conversation starters and chat to break the silence of what had just happened.

While I was looking at these things, she said 'I have some specific things I want to show you later.' I was being a good guest and let her be a good host. Trying to step back and let her take the lead, respecting her and her house. She started blurting out the things she wanted to do such as having favourite activities around the house and especially in her bedroom. Things started to get a bit awkward, but I pretended as if I was not paying attention. The shed was one thing but inside the house was another. So of course, I started to suggest things to do that did not involve the bedroom. She said 'don't worry you will be fine, you don't need to be shy'. I was then thinking is she normal?

'Are you going to do what I ask?' she said with a strong voice

I said 'what are you asking?'

'I said let's go to the bedroom' she replied

I was standing right next to the sofa. She looked at me and said 'I really like you, why are so difficult? When I first saw you, you brought so much joy and beauty into my life since we met.'

I was standing there thinking 'this girl is crazy.'

I stood there, frozen in one place. My mind was racing. I knew I wanted to say yes, just to keep her happy, but my brain was trying to caution me. I chose to ignore everything that I was thinking. So I looked down at her and said 'yes, let's do whatever you plan to do.'

She got up and dragged me by my hand into her bedroom.

When I got in the bedroom, she already had everything set out. My name was written on one of the pillows and her name on the other. I said to myself 'I cannot imagine what is going on in this girl's head at the moment or what the hell she was thinking.'

When I got into the bedroom, she looked at me with a wide smile and said 'will you please do me the honour by helping me take off my clothes?'

Then all of a sudden she started to cry. 'Are you alright?' I asked.

She said 'Yes, I am crying because I am very happy.'

'Happy for what?' I asked.

'You are in my bedroom' she said with a soft voice.

At this point, this was becoming something I will never forget in my whole life as long as I live. It was unforgettable.

As I was in the process of taking of her clothes, she said 'you are making me so happy.'

I said 'OK'

She turned around and said 'we are both happy – right?'.

I said 'at least one of us is.'

She was very persistent so she was not taking no for answer and she believed she had the right to impose herself on me. Even though I say she was crazy, do not misunderstand me: she was damned crazy. I do not think this whole visit was to study, it was too well arranged. Despite what I said, she already made up her mind what she wanted to do in her heart and soul.

We both lay on the bed facing each other. She appeared settled and enjoyed spending time with me. She explained that she was very anxious when she initially joined the team at the company but as soon as she saw me she knew she wanted me, so she was looking forward to come in to work every day. The support and the welcome she received from me, helped her to overcome her barriers including supporting her with her anxiety, lack of skills, and low mood. To be honest, all that went over my head. I could not remember all that. I believe she was making things up in her head as she went along.

While lying there I was thinking, I just want this girl to make a decision about when she will start studying and get on with it. I tried to change the conversation a bit and said that I believed she was very intelligent and had the ability to do whatever she wanted, not knowing she took that the wrong way.

She jumped on top of me, and said 'yes you are right'. I really thought I was making the situation better by telling her that I was there to support her. I really did not know that she would take it that way. She was behaving as if she was feeling lonely and was desperate to be wanted.

She took that opportunity to start her sex activities and yes I participated to make her happy. I was scared not to make the situation any worse as she was in the flow.

Even so, I was young and still in my teens and this whole experience was a big slap in the face. All of a sudden, I realized that this girl was damn spoiled and she always had it her way. I felt like an idiot, even though I was trying to behave with a certain level of maturity. This was hard for me, because I had never met anyone like this before. It was an experience I would never forget. I'd been able to do whatever I wanted to a certain degree but not like this, with the way her behaviour was. She was able to turn on a dime and go in any direction. And I was still trying!

Sometimes I think I have too much energy for my own good and just like staying busy for no good reason. Here I am looking to make something of myself and be stable and choosing to have gratitude for how this crazy journey was unfolding before me.

I felt burnt out physically and emotionally and I kept saying to myself that 'this is normal.' I needed to take a break. I would probably not succeed at anything if I continued like this. I needed to start on a new path. I needed to know myself better, understand the situation I was getting into, and the amount of time I needed before my next big burst of energy into doing something good for the future. But not this.

I had to believe that there was exponentially more opportunity in the present moment than there ever had been in my past. Even those big moments I thought I missed. I believed that was my mind playing tricks on me. My past, like the present, really is an illusion.

I took a snap shot while I was there in that house of my situation right there and then and saw I could make some decisions without letting the past or the future blind me. I was struggling with this every day.

It had been a few hours. It was getting very late, and I needed to go. So I got up, got dressed and said 'I have to go now.'

She said 'do you have to leave?'

'Yes' I replied

She then said 'I have a confession, you are my spouse, partner, friend and my expectations match yours.'

I said 'what does that mean?'

'I am determining to invest more time with you and I want wake up with you right next to me', she replied.

In return I said 'Let me think about it and get back to you.'

It seemed like I pushed her buttons. She got so angry and said 'you are not leaving me, I am not letting you go.'

She was cracking. She was really lashing out. I felt so uncomfortable with what I was seeing and the way she was behaving, I felt like I was held captive. So it got me thinking 'what the hell is going on here?' I was sitting there and thinking about different ways of dealing with this situation. I was trying to have this dialogue with her, but it seemed things were getting from bad to worse. I didn't get why she was flipping in this way. What pressure have I put myself into?

I tried not talking and give her the silent treatment, but it didn't work. She kept saying 'I am talking to you.'

I said 'but I am listening.'

'You are ignoring my feelings' she said.

This was getting harder for me to process. At this point I just wanted to disappear.

'What are you saying exactly?' I asked.

'I like you. You are my first' she said.

I did not understand at that present moment what that meant.

She was a lonely child I was feeling like a lonely child. We both needed some attention. We both gave each other some fulfilment (well….I think I did). I wasn't too sure what her aspirations were, or what her priorities were, nor what she wanted to achieve in that short space of time knowing each other but this was not looking good in my eyes.

It was getting very late. Everyone would want to know what was going on with me and where I was. I just wanted to get out of that house because I knew what else was to come when I got home with my sister's father.

She kept using some sort of emotional blackmail. She said that if I left she was going to scream and tell people that I raped her. My life was now full of fear, I had to work extra hard emotionally to calm her down and make some kind of obligation and the guilt I was feeling afterward was making me sick.

I said 'don't worry, I promise I will come back and see you. I have to do something'

She had hidden my shoes so I asked her 'where are my shoes?' She said 'I don't know. Somewhere.'

She was using all kind of things to manipulate me. This was the tactic she was using to keep me there. She was an obsessed person, an abuser threatening me with everything to get what she wanted. There came a point when it was making me feel fear, anger, and guilt all at the same time. She wanted to have things all her way. I was trying so hard to refuse to take responsibility for her actions but instead I blamed myself for going there in the first place.

I said to her 'Its ok it's my fault. I am to blame for all of this, it was a very bad decision I made. I am very sorry.'

It's relatively easy to persist when things are going well and we see progress but highly persistent people have find ways to keep going despite major setbacks and a lack of evidence that they are moving closer toward their goals. She was very persistent in what she wanted. This woman had a goal and vision in her mind that was motivating and driving her. I noticed she was a dreamer and visionary who saw her life as having a higher purpose than simply taking one step at a time. Her vision to have me twenty-four-seven was deeply ingrained and she had been focusing on it constantly and with great emotion and energy.

With her spoiled attitude and having her own way, together with her persistence, she made it clear that she wanted it bad, really bad, and she was not looking for an excuse or a way out.

I left without my shoes, took my bike and off I went home to meet another situation.

I left there with such a speed, I had no clue as to where I was going as it was dark. I got home, slowly slid the door open and quietly stepped in the house. I managed to sneak into my room only to find my sister's father sitting on my bed.

'Where were you?' he said.

'I was helping one of my work colleagues with her preparation for her exams' I replied.

He put his hands around me and said 'we were worried.' I said 'there was no need to be worried I am here now. You can tell everyone that they don't have to worry about me' I said.

He tried to do a sexual act on me and said 'I have a gift for you.' I pushed him away and said 'can you leave the room please? You think you know me, but you don't. From what I have seen, I am still not convinced of what kind of person you are, and without any offence meant, I don't want to know all of your darkest secrets.' You say you have a gift, you can keep your gift for someone else. I am not interested. Now get out.'

He said 'you are mad, completely crazy or you're drunk'. I said 'No, I am just pissed off, and I am not in any mood for any nonsense.'

He said to me 'I have taken on the role as a father to you, and this is not what I thought would happen.'

I looked at him and said 'really?' Sorry to disappoint you.'

While I was coming to terms with who he really was, I was doing my best within the home, and I had good intentions to be a son and a brother to my sister. I did not want to feel left out or make anyone upset or use my sister against me. But this was very hurtful and perplexing for me at the time.

I spoke with him that evening, and I said 'I know how much you are doing for me and you have taken the role as a father in my life, but you are not giving me anything to respect you as a father.' I continued by saying 'you are not respecting my boundaries. I am not your lover, I am supposed to be your step-son. I had so many people who took on the role of a father in my life and your image of a father in this family is not what I expect of you. This is leaving me a bit confused and hurt.'

I tried so hard to build a level of trust, love and care with the family, but sometimes I had feelings of hurt and anger towards them. Every time I acted out and I was feeling a loss of control, I would go out and find something to do such as hanging out with friends. Every time I did that he would throw his hands up in the air and say, 'I cannot take this one more day'!

Turbulence was getting between me and him in the form of me acting out, being defiance, talking back, and not adhering to what he wanted me to do. Rarely was my childhood evolved or mature enough to handle the complex feelings that came from being in a stepfamily.

My sister came home for the weekend and saw that I was not happy. She asked 'what's the matter?' I said 'nothing, I am fine' but she continued to question me, so I explained to her what had happened, but I did not tell her how her father tried to throw himself at me sexually, and how terrible I was feeling.

I said to her 'Are there any suggestions on how to handle this situation?' She told me to apologise to him, not because I did anything wrong but just to keep the peace because she did not want to lose me as a brother. She wanted me to stay. I said 'I will have to earn his trust and that could take years and years. Give me a break! Why should I bother?'

When I was immersed in my teenager life, I struggled inwardly to feel successful, valued and to make what I felt was a positive contribution in the world. Back then, I thought I was brave, but I wasn't. Not by a long shot. I was afraid all the time, and I didn't muster the courage to speak up and stand up for myself, or for others. I didn't have the strength to take on that which was wrong and unfair, glaring me right in the face. I was afraid of not being liked if I showed my true feelings. I was deeply afraid that I never really knew enough to "belong" there in a powerful way (some kind of imposter syndrome played big tricks with my head).

That evening I had managed to figure out the way to muster the bravery to step beyond that hardship and stood up to her. I spoke up more boldly, stood up courageously for myself and when I did, it changed everything. I didn't see her again for a while. About a month later I went to a birthday party. I looked up from my drink and my eyes met hers where she stood in the light of the doorway but only for a fraction of a second. In that moment I felt a hot arrow, invisible and quick as lighting, pass right through my chest. It almost jolted me out of seat. I felt my heart thumping.

She was smiling and waving at a woman sitting by the table next to me. It had been almost a month since I last saw her. I must say that she was beautiful and stunning that evening. Seeing her, a torrent of memories came rushing over me, I felt beads of sweat on my forehead, a familiar knot in my stomach.

I wondered whether she recognised me, but I knew in that very brief moment when our eyes met, she must have seen that it was me. She sat by her friend at the table to the right of me and I realised I probably wouldn't be able to eat with my heart in my throat. 'But you're grown up now', a voice inside me said, 'relax.'

I wasn't sure what would happen next, but going on past records if I wasn't very careful, it could be life-altering. I couldn't rationalise my feelings in that moment, but intuitively I felt that if I turned and reached across the space between us I would cross and entangle the sacred timelines that had kept us apart for so long; that if I looked too deeply into her eyes, we would alter the course of events, and in so doing affect the future.

I didn't turn right, I didn't look back. I calmly stood up and walked towards the light. I had chosen my path a long time ago. There was no way to go back to undo the things we did and said. So I slung my bag over my shoulder and picked up my drink as I strolled into the sunshine, keenly aware that her eyes were following me with questions as I left the room.

CHAPTER EIGHT

Another Path

I have learned over the years even from a young age to admire people who seem to know where they are going in life. This was telling me that setting goals in life is an important life skill. I have heard people repeat maxims such as "You can't hit a target you haven't set up" or "If you don't know where you're going, any road will take you there".

I wanted to find a path for myself. I knew that there was some value to setting goals for myself but I was discovering that it wasn't really as critical as some people thought it was. In those days, when people asked me about my life, I often responded, 'I am grateful to be alive, thank you.' I didn't mean to be flippant; I simply wanted to emphasise that to me the important issue was how I lived my life, and not just the goal.

Seeing that I couldn't become a pharmacist, I decided to become a male nurse to caring for people so I signed up for some evening classes. I had spoken with a doctor and he recommended a course for me. I did some research and I got myself an application form, filled it out and off I went. This was becoming my career path.

The first day I arrived, there were about twenty five students in the classroom and all were women. With such a small male-to-female ratio in this industry, at some point on a typical day a man in this industry often sees himself alone in a room full of women. The first time I saw this and what was happening, I realised that this industry was for mainly for young women in this educational path. In my head I was thinking this could have a tremendous effect on how I view myself, and my place in it.

The first day I arrived in the class, the male teacher said to me 'a warm welcome. Welcome to the honey pot.' In reply I said 'thank you' but I was also thinking again, how did I get here?

It was a very large classroom, there were lots of seats, so I chose to sit at the very back of the classroom. I took out my empty exercise book, and a pen out of my bag. All ready to go. But I was also thinking 'can I possibly do this and pass this class?'

I sat there quietly, looking around, minding my own business waiting for the professor to start. There was this woman sitting to my right who introduced herself to me. She was a beautiful, curly-haired woman with long eyelashes and a gentle demeanor. She said 'how does it feel sitting here in this class with all these women?' I said 'it's still early days.' I was hoping that another male would join us at some point.

The woman next to me said that she was there because there was a court order and the judge made her take up a study class so she chose this one.

After the lesson was finished, we were both walking out together, and I said 'I am very interested in your story.'

She began by telling me: I got married very young in my culture, and I did not like him, he was no match for me. As a matter of fact I started to hate him, but I had no choice but to go ahead with the marriage because that was the culture.

After a year or so I was hoping that I would get to like and maybe love him but he did not give me any reason to like him and definitely love was out of the question, so I started to hate him even more. He was under pressure from his side of the family to have kids and my side of the family did not help the situation either.

I tried so hard not to have sex with him. I kept making up excuses after excuses. One day he came home drunk and he raped me. (In those days while you were married, husbands did not rape their wife. In the community's eyes, he was taking what was his). I could not tell anyone because no cared about what happened within a marriage. I got pregnant and that made the whole family except for me jump for joy because I knew that this was not how my child should be born. (By a raping husband)

During my pregnancy I used to feel low most of the time and it was affecting my life. Some days I did not know what to do with myself. I thought maybe I would go to my parent's house and stay a few hours just to clear my head. A few hours became a few days and my father said that I should not be coming to their house anymore because I had a husband to look after. She said I tried talking to my mother, to let her know how I was feeling about the situation, but she did not want to know. All she kept saying was 'it will get better'. I started drinking my husband's drink so I could fall asleep when he arrived home. That was the only thing I could do to cope. I had no support and I was finding it hard to cope. Some days I was just in a low mood, feeling mad and sad with the whole world. Other days I was angry and frustrated.

At times I wish I had someone to talk to about what my options were. It had crossed my mind so many times to have an abortion. I wished I had an option where there was a space to think through things through away from my inside pressures of the family. Sometimes my feelings were up and sometimes down, every day was different and I did not know what the best decision for me was. I just wanted to be free to talk to someone in confidence.

I was young and was not ready for marriage or to have a baby. Dealing with an unplanned pregnancy and with all this drama I was surely considering an abortion as a solution to my situation. My mother was not there to talk me through what to do. I got married and that was that. No one cared anymore and I was thinking about my health and well-being and I wanted to know the facts about having a baby.

Abortion was not just a simple procedure. To me it was a life changing event with all the significant physical, emotional, and spiritual consequences that came with it and I was not ready for that.

One day while I drank myself to sleep, he came home drunk and he raped me again. This time it felt worse than before. He put his hands over my mouth and said 'you are my wife and I will have this whenever I want.' I woke up because I couldn't breathe. All I was feeling was his penis inside of me. I said to him 'stop you are hurting me' he said 'you are wrong, that is what sex is all about'. I said 'this is rape'. He said 'stop being stupid, husbands do not rape their wives.'

As soon as I got up and left the bed, I went to the toilet, and there I realised that I was bleeding. I came out the toilet with tears in my eyes and he saw me, but I did not look at him. He realised what he had done. He held my hands and said 'I'm so sorry' as realisation crept into the lines across his forehead. 'Please, I'm so sorry.' By him touching me I felt sick, so I ran into the bathroom and brought everything up.

It was the beginning of what would be months of apologies. He wrote a note an hour later to apologise again because I was not going to speak to him. An hour after that he wrote another note saying that he was sorry. By this time he was sobering up. I took every note he wrote and folded it up and put it in my note book. I didn't respond to anything he was saying to me.

That day I wasn't too sure what went wrong, but while I was sitting at my desk in my bedroom I started crying. He kept apologising to me profusely and he told me he'd never do it again. He knew what he did wrong. He didn't mean to hurt me. What more could I ask for? I thought. As he tearily begged for my forgiveness, suddenly my heart broke. This was the first time he had ever asked for forgiveness. This means he's different, right? This means it's OK.

I got up and lay myself on the bed. He came over and give me a hug and a kiss on my forehead. He kept rubbing my arms and playing with my hair. He was not saying anything so I closed my eyes and found myself halfway between pleasure and confusion. I always thought of orgasms like a hurricane, with all my nerves twisting and turning and rising up out of my body.

This time I was having some form of denial. So many things were going through my head just lying there with him right next to me. A thought came into my head to start self-harming to deal with the trauma. I wanted to be self-destructive. I was full of anger and self-loathing. I got up and when to the bathroom, took all my clothes off and took one of his razors and cut into my thighs. I took painfully cold showers, and scratched my skin open. I was then bleeding all over the place but I did not care anymore.

While I was in the bathroom all I was thinking was this man is a rapist and a monster. Maybe this was why I didn't expect to feel or have any human feelings for him. In some ways, those feelings were a form of denial. When I scrubbed away my memories of the assault, what remained was the non-attraction I'd felt toward him before.

A few weeks later, guess what? He did it again. Came home drunk and he tried to rape me again. This time for some reason I was ready and prepared for him because I had the feeling it was going to happen again. When he arrived in the room I knew that something was wrong and he was up to something. The way he looked at me made me feel like I was his sex meat. But not this time! I got up straight away, went to the kitchen and took a knife and hid it in my panties.

On the way back from the kitchen, he grabbed me from behind, leaned me over the table with his pants down ready to pounce on me. So I took the knife, turned around, grabbed his penis and said 'one more move and this will be the last time you ever see or use this'.

He thought I was joking, I was so full of anger and rage I did not care what happened next. All I knew was I was going to cut that damn penis off that evening. He started to laughed and said 'and what are you going to do with that'? The more he laughed, the more the anger was raging inside of me. He took his hands and tried to them put around my neck and there he had it! I sliced it off completely. He fell to the floor and I stood there just looking at him with a smile. All I heard him saying was 'Call the ambulance'. I saw his mouth moving, but none of his words were registering.

As we were walking and she was explaining to me what had

happened, I was listening to every word and was thinking in my head 'Oh my goodness – he really drove you to mental insanity'.

She continued: The police and the ambulance came, not sure who called them. The only thing I could remember was my parents came to the police station, did not even talk to me about getting bail or to find out what had happened, or at least hear my side of the story. My father just looked at me and said I had disgraced the family. The things he said at the police station were very hurtful and even the staff at the station were shocked and surprised that a father could say such a thing to his daughter. They had now disowned me. Why was I surprised? They never believed me anyway. They won't even know the truth even if it was staring at them in the face.

I went to court, and the judge sentenced me to five years in prison for attempted murder. I did not have a lawyer, because I couldn't afford one. The day I went to court was one of the most frightening things of my life. Right there and then he looked at me and said five years. I still believe to this day that my dad or his parents paid the judge. Everyone with money knows each other in this town.

That evening we kept walking until we ending up in park. I put my bike down and we both sat down and continued talking. She continued to say:

My life turned upside down the day I arrived in prison. I was only nineteen years old then and my cell mates did their best to bully me in everywhere possible. None of them knew I was pregnant. After the first week, these girls attacked me in the shower and they beat the hell out of me. I started to bleed again and unfortunately I lost the baby. Since that day I didn't care what happened next. I started misbehaving at a lot. I just didn't care. I got excluded a lot from that wing and I got kicked out of that prison for good, then I moved to another prison which was a bit quieter and calmer so I would sit all by myself in a corner and not speak to anyone for about a month. I would just sit there until it was time to go back to my cell.

One of my cell mates had a friend on the outside who used to visit every week and supplied anything she needed. So I started drinking and smoking hash nearly every day just to numb the pain I was feeling inside. Then after about a year, I started taking ecstasy followed by coke. I had no one to visit me or to give me money, so I found a job inside the prison and when my cell-mate and I had enough money we would order more stuff.

After another year, I started to have a nervous breakdown. I wasn't myself anymore. I sat in my regular corner and then suddenly I found myself speaking calmly and gently, discussing some of the most traumatic events of my life to myself.

After the death of my unborn baby, I went through a severe post-natal depression (PND), which went undiagnosed. They called the doctor and she linked it directly to the long-term domestic abuse from my violent ex-partner.

My depression, coupled with an increasing dependence on alcohol, led to my mental breakdown. The doctor went back to the judge and told him what was happening to me. The judge called me back to his court room and wanted to charge me with child neglect and abandonment, all because I did not mention that I was pregnant at the time of my sentence. My world literally caved in around my ears. I said to the judge 'I felt like a terrible human. I had let myself, my unborn baby and everyone down.' I pleaded guilty to everything.

The doctor said 'This woman is experiencing hell while there, she was given no support for her addiction or her mental ill health, and it would have a dramatic impact on the following months. Your honour I don't believe that prison will be good for her.' The judge looked at me and said 'do you have somewhere to live'?

My cell mate spoke to her friend and recommended that friend to me as they had place where I could live for a while. However, the judge added another term and condition. He said 'you have to take up a study course that comes with a qualification. Studying for professional qualifications can help you develop the skills you need to impress employers in your chosen job or industry, and for some careers they are essential for your next step in life.'

While I was sitting in my cell, it got me thinking. I had to find a vocational training course that related to a specific industry or career path that I was interested in. I had not finished school and I had no university degree. This would take me several years of studying but I needed it for myself. While I was in prison, I had seen many women and each story was different. There is no one type of woman who experiences unwanted pregnancy. I saw everyone from victims of rape and abuse, to women who knew there was a fetal abnormality. Some were very well educated, others were illiterate, some were Muslim, others were Catholic, some were young and others were in their 40s. I needed the experience so I could develop my career further. So here we are that's my story and that's why I ended up on this course.

I held her hands and asked 'how are you doing now?'

She said 'well I am now in a better place, and I just want to build my life again.'

I then looked at her and said 'Some people may feel totally fine to talk to you nicely in front of your face, but behind your back they say something else. Don't worry, you can get through it. I know it can feel extremely uncomfortable talking about things and with the anxiety, all of this can bring up a lot of emotions'.

I continued by saying to her 'everyone has a story to tell, sometimes you feel like you have to explain your life choices to others. Perhaps you're worried about what others are thinking and whether they'll judge you for your decision to make a change and/or what you have chosen to pursue now.'

I also said to her 'we can become friends and we can get through this course together. We can help each other if you want to. You may feel pretty strongly that you know what others are thinking and have in their mind that they're judging you and your career change in some negative light, but unless they explicitly tell you, you can never really know for sure. So, until you do know for sure, put your conjectures aside. What others are thinking is their business, not yours.'

We became very good friends, we helped each other and we got through the first year. In the same way we took and exchanged notes when attending the lectures. We decided it was a good idea to do the same while listening to and watching the video lectures. We sat in a comfortable place both in the classroom and sometimes in the park, having our notebook and pen handy and tried to keep any other distractions to a minimum. We also made sure that we had the same timetable and worked out our study schedule to ensure we were well-prepared to attend all the seminars and lectures. We did all the relevant reading beforehand and asked questions if there was anything we were not sure about.

I told her we needed to stay focused. We had to give it our best shot. So we studied hard for that class, learning the subject backwards and forwards, working through every problem in the books. We both were overcompensating for this feeling that we had some sort of disadvantage. As a result we got the highest grades in the class in the first year, and in the process we became hooked on all the subjects. We saw the maths that we loved in a new light as it so beautifully guided our understanding of the fundamental part of the course.

We got to know each other as good friends. We kept talking about everything and anything. I was getting very attached to her. One day we had lots of studying to do, and I couldn't go to her place, all because of her restrictions from the judge and her housemate was not going to be happy with that. She was afraid to get herself into trouble and the park was not really a good idea, because the weather was not so great that week. It was the rainy season.

We decided to take another path and come to my place instead, which at the time was a great idea, all because I wanted to prove a point to my sister's father that I was only interested in women and not men. This was the best way to prove that. So without letting him know, I brought her round to my place.

From an early age I was told that there's someone out there for everyone, it's just a matter of finding them and the moment I do, my life will change forever. It's a lovely thought, but growing up, I didn't believe a word of it.

As a teenager, all I cared about at this stage was the next big achievement in my next chapter of life. Here I was thinking maybe this woman would be my guarding angel or maybe we could achieve it together. Don't get me wrong, I wasn't looking to leave a trail of broken hearts behind me, I wanted to settle down in my studies and start making something of my life.

She came over, we got a soft drink and sat on the balcony because it was hot inside the house, and off we went into our studies. After about an hour, it started to rain and we began to get wet, so we decided to grab our books and return inside in the front room. No one was at home. My sister's father was out of town that day and was expected back late that afternoon and my sister was at her grandmother. We were all alone.

While sitting next to her, I looked over at her and suddenly I saw this beautiful woman sitting next to me. This woman with curly dark hair and the most amazing smile. I was transfixed and for the next few minutes, I couldn't take my eyes off her as she absentmindedly tucked a stray curl behind her ear, then threw back her head and laughed. 'Why are you looking at me' she said. 'Nothing' I replied.

She then kissed me on the cheek and smiled. It's true that being kissed is a big deal, but it can mean different things based on the situation. That kiss felt good. I did not want to spoil this relationship I had with this woman. Although this might sound confusing, I said to myself I will try holding her hands first to clarify if this is what she wants so I will know exactly what I needed to do.

There was silence as we kept looking at each other as I held her hands. She'd been using the time to think the same way I was really thinking. I believe it was time for her to bounce back from everything and become the best version of herself. She began to give in to temptation to reach out to me, even though she wanted to hold back with her heart. I broke the silence by saying 'we have been friends for a long time now and I don't want to spoil this friendship we have'. She said 'I know … and I want to us to remain friends too'.

She told me that she recognised that and saw that I did too and that she was doing what was in her power to make sure that she didn't spoil our friendship too. I don't want to end up doing the same thing with my life a second time. I asked her if she had made any changes as well, and she replied that she actually started thinking of me for a while and she was hoping that I was feeling the same and hoping that I would make the first move and she was willing to do whatever to help motivate me. Anyway, we continued talking and the next thing

I knew we were having a passionate kiss on the sofa. She then pushed me away and ran to the toilet, and after a few minutes she came back with no panties on. And there we go….. We had our first sex session after months of friendship. Everything we did was very passionate. I felt that I did not have sex with her, I made love to her.

There were clear signs that we were on the right track and we continued to see each other secretly for about three years. We both qualified. Unfortunately, she had to move to another town which was about five hours drive away because of her family, and we lost contact. I have never seen her again. I was kind of heart broken.

CHAPTER NINE

Contemplation

Life is an aging process. Each day passes and we don't know what to expect the next day. All of us will go through it in our own way. How we lead our lives as we get older, particularly as we near the end, is worth pondering. In this way getting some good news and some bad news help us to learn: Then we contemplate and make decisions with which way our life will take us.

Have you ever had a good idea but didn't have the time or energy to do anything with it? I knew that my biological mother lived here in this country for a few years. There must be some of her personal friends who still lived here that can fill in the gaps for me.

I was invited to a family party one evening and I was considering if I should go or not. To be honest I wasn't feeling up to it. My sister came over that weekend and convinced me that I should go, all because she needed company and she wanted to show off to her friends that I was her brother.

I knew that some of the people that were going to be there knew all about the situation (sex life) my sister's father was secretly having and they were going to look at me in a funny way, thinking I was one of his playboys. However, I thought about it and found the way and courage and the bravery to go. I addressed and moved through my fears, revised my feelings of unworthiness, and overcame my concerns about feeling a bit rejected in such a gathering. Isolating myself and having bad feelings for these people was not going to help the situation.

It was time to stop seeing myself in the old, habitual, small way. I told myself this would be a new story that makes me the hero of my life, and not the loser. Understanding what and who has formed and influenced me from the past, but knowing that those influences are *from the past* and it will not continue to hold me down. Only I can shape my future differently, right now. I needed to pull myself up by the bootstraps, move beyond my current challenges and hardships and embrace all that I am to start stepping up towards my highest vision.

I needed to understand the dominant way I could take action towards my goal and what I needed to motivate myself to move forward and start leveraging my dominant style more fully. I needed to stop pretending to be someone I was not. Forget that. I just needed to recognise who I was at my core and I was willing to start honouring it.

I arrived at the party, and there were lots of people gathered there. Many of them knew my sister's father and also knew who I was but I'd never seen nearly half of them before.

For some reason most of the time it seemed to me that the moment I had to meet people for the first time was the legit scariest thing I had to do as a teenager. That was a terrifying experience but I kept telling myself "it really doesn't have to be". At first, my intention was not to talk to anyone, because in my heart I just had those bad feelings about everyone. But I snapped myself out of it and told myself 'The important thing is to just be yourself. Plus, once the first meeting is out of the way, it only gets easier'.

I was standing in a corner with my sister having a bit of a conversation from one thing to another. Then this woman walked up to me. She looked like someone I had seen before. She said hello to my sister. They hugged and greeted each other. Then she turned to me and said, 'You can't remember me'. I said 'maybe from somewhere'. She said 'I am the niece of your adopted mother'.

I learned growing up that my adopted mother had a sister who had many children (eleven) and the family of my adopted mother was very upset because she took me instead of taking some of her sister's children. One did came to live with her before I was born, and this niece was the one, but she left when she was a teenager. I don't even know if we would ever have been told what happen next.

I learned that evening at the party that for some years my adopted mother and her sister never spoke for many years all because of that situation. My adopted mother tried to keep in touch with her, but her sister refused. Eventually, she must have had to make the heart-breaking decision to give up.

This has not been talked about openly within the family. I had no idea how much contact my adopted mother had with her siblings and their children and, to my knowledge from what she was telling me, my adopted mother had not seen her since she left. I realised early on that it was a subject considered off limits, though I did clumsily try to find out more in that conversation.

I knew nothing much about my adopted mother's family, apart from some of their names, and had never felt any real desire to meet them. However, I never had any need to have to contact them. But this was about to change. I shied away from family conflict and I had always assumed it would be me who would be left out.

I said to her 'I found it intriguing that this has never been talked about before by any of them, not even between you and your family. Families are great places to keep secrets, aren't they'?

She told me her history of coming over to this country. And how much she knew my mother while she was still living there in that country. And when and how my sister was born.

She called me over to one side and said 'the first thing that you should work out, is how to make contact with your mother. Get yourself out from this family.' I then said to her 'where should I start? Do you where she is?' If she wanted to help, these were really important questions. I knew that too often, people go into complicated family situations without analysing what it is they really want or how to achieve it. I wanted to make sure I was doing the right thing.

She said 'I knew where she was all along, but I kept it quiet' I said 'oh, and why it is such a secret?' She then said 'It's a long story. It's history'

She continued by saying 'when you have a good think about what I have said, you would end up with the answers and then work backwards, you might have a better idea of how to go about this. You have to make things better for yourself. Do you want to get closer and get to know your mum? This can reunite everyone.'

Then she continued to speak about another friend my mother had who worked at a bar in the city. They all came to the country together. This news made my eyes open even wider and inspired me to know more about this historical event. I might be able to discover more about my biological mother from their story and might be able to connect with this other friend. This was a breakthrough, as I was struggling with so many unanswered questions, so all of this was now capturing my attention.

I did not want us to drift apart. I took her contacts (address), and I was looking forward for more information and having more conversations about this. We arranged to get together again. The one person who I needed the most, there was now a breakthrough, and I thought I could do what I could to get to the bottom of this. At first when I heard it I got a bit upset, angry and a little confused. What had I done so wrong? – Why had none of my sister's family ever spoken to me about this?

I was exploring ways to dissect my life and take it all in, so that one day I may either enjoy life in a deeper sense or glean famous "life lessons" more easily.

The answer was "No." then "Yes" The question was, am I really ready and truly ready to experience what I was about to hear? The best thing I had do was to admit that I was looking for something to put my mind at ease, and instead try to validate everything for myself.

I set my mind to ask and accept questions and answers, so I could receive within myself this distinctly internal adventure. Recognising that the most hated things in my life was not knowing and not being *loved* by the person who brought me into this world, but I still hated the unknown (all mixed-up) because these were the things that held me back from keeping an open-mind.

One day I took my bike and I made the effort and I went to see this friend that was working at the bar in the city. I walked in and she looked at me and said 'Oh my goodness, I never thought I would see this day.'

The bar was fully packed with people and I looked around, because I wasn't sure if she was talking to me. She said 'I need a strong drink. I just can't believe my eyes'.

When I arrived, our eyes locked together. In my head I was thinking 'Why am I here? What is my purpose here?' and 'am I ready to fulfil this purpose?' The chain of questions was actually never ending. I was thinking of it as a rope I was climbing but I was never reaching the top - yet the farther I go upward, the better the view to see the boulders on the ground below becomes.

I sat down on one of the stools at the bar, and she poured me a beer, and said 'this deserves a drink'. She yelled out my name and said 'is that you?'

I didn't understand why everyone was so secretive regarding my biological mother – anything but – so my imaginations went crazy and in the worst possible places. It felt strange and disorientating to be all of a sudden contemplating a situation of such gravity: why hadn't anyone told me what the situation was all about? It seemed this was a big secret. Everyone knew about it except me. But I was hoping to get some kind of answers.

There were no pictures of my biological mother around. I had no memories of her to reflect on and there were no conversations about her to bring her to mind. All I ever knew was I had a non-biological mother, and it was the same for most my childhood.

I don't think I was ever mad at her for not being there, nor did I hold any grudges. I really was just indifferent to the idea of ever knowing her.

I never heard much about the type of person she was. All I really knew was that she wasn't there, and didn't contribute to my life and upbringing. So now being there at the bar, hoping to get some kind of answer or something, to put my mind at ease, I just wanted to leave there with something, so I could go away hoping to get something to help me understand.

CHAPTER TEN

Contemplation: The life story

Understanding the pattern-seeking mind is the first step toward real wisdom

Day one

She began to me tell the story.

A big part of my life was knowing your mother. We met from the age of fifteen and we were friends ever since, both in the good times and the bad times. Whether it is family love, relationship love or friendship love.

Your adopted mother was the one who brought up your mother. Her father was not married to her mother (my grandmother) who was from an Indian background, because her family did not approve of the relationship between the two cultures.

During the pregnancy, her mother did not want her family to know. So she ran away from her family and when the baby was born she took the baby to your grandfather. He was too busy with his work and did not have the time to look after the baby. She did not want to keep the baby, because she had no funds to look after the baby and the family would not have accepted her and the baby from a father with a different background and to top it all off they were not married.

In those days, such thing was a death penalty from the Indian family.

She left the baby on the doorstep at her father's place, and ran away, never to be seen again. So the father came home and found the baby at the doorstep, picked the baby up and put the child in his car and drove about four hours to a friend he knew for many years.

My adopted mother and her husband were very good friends to my grandfather.

He arrived and explained to them that because of his work commitments he did not have the time to look after this baby. They did not have any children of their own, so they were happy to take the child in and look after her. He did promise to return to collect the child at some point. But that did not happen. Not sure if he supported financially in any way.

My biological mother lived there from the age of two days old until she was fifteen and ran away from the home. No one knew where she had gone and how to find her.

To me it was very important to pay attention to the story as it was becoming real and I did not want anything to be missed or let it pass by. It was also the reality of how my life occurred to me in any given moment. All of this was giving me more perspective on life and now I was feeling more at peace. I was conscious of the time, but I wanted to hear more but it was getting a bit late. I left and said 'we have to continue this another day.'

Day two

This was the story that had the power behind my life. For me it was important to trust her for the things she was about to say, and try and work out and put the dots together the best way I could possibly imagine, irrespective of what I thought. So I returned to get as much information as possible.

She continued

I met your mother at a night club, and we became friends ever since. We were both were fifteen. I was a runaway child too. In those days parents were very strict. I had a falling out with my mother, because my step father tried to rape me while I was sleeping one evening. I told my mother and she did not believe me and she did nothing. So one evening when he came into my room, I was pretending I was sleeping and I had a knife next to me in my bed. When he came in and sat down next to me, I pushed him, jumped out of the bed and ran away and I am still running today. I never looked back. I never made contact with my mother ever again.

I went to a friend, who was in the same position I was, and I stayed there for a few months. I then met a guy who liked me and I moved out from the friend's house and stayed with him. When I met your mother at the night club she came back to my place and we all stayed together in this small little house.

From the very first time I met your mother we were like sisters. We never kept secrets from each other. She told me that that this supposed boyfriend was trying to hit on her. I went crazy and I wanted to kill him that day. I packed my bags and I left and of course your mother followed.

There was a ferry station where you could take a boat that went from one end of the village to another town so we both went to the ferry station and stood there and decided what to do next. This guy came up to us and asked us what our names were. He looked very rich and he said we could both stay at his place. We were young and stupid and maybe desperate for somewhere to stay.

He had his own businesses and one of them was a bar. We both got a job at his place, serving and flirting with customers. What I did at work pretty much revolved around men doing what I loved to do with the people I met. In other words, we both were looking for someone to love us. Love made my world go round, and without love, I would not even want to exist on this planet. We both were taught that making friendships with the customers is what made them come back and spend money. The importance of friendship, is what has helped me in life, and my long quest for a lasting love which we were both looking for, would later on became our major problem.

The rich guy was only using us to make money by letting us work at the bar for free. One of the things I remember was we both wanted and were thinking the same thing, even though we were uniquely different. We both had different gifts and skills, different ways of thinking and being. We were most definitely "fearfully and wonderfully made" and we were determined to find someone who was willing to love us.

We were so desperately looking for anyone who we believed was willing to give us that attention. I did so much for everyone in my life yet I felt used and taken for granted. We chased love in many directions yet rarely felt fulfilled. Sometimes, some of these men that came into the bar would use us like a door-mat. We both sacrificed our own needs, and happiness, to make others happy, believing that they'd love us for it. It took us a while of hurting and complaining and yearning to each other for love to realise that nothing we did for others made us feel loved.

I have a word of advice for you "self-love is the beginning of a wonderful loving life". If you want love in your life, go to the mirror and say, 'I will make the effort to be more loving to you, starting today! Even if you don't love yourself, say it with feeling. Do it whenever you can.' It started with our consciousness raising about doing loving things for us and not for other people.

One evening it was a bit quiet at the bar and we noticed two gentlemen walk in who said 'we would like to order our drinks at the far corner of the bar.' One of them was pointing where he wanted the drinks. These were old men, but nicely dressed and well spoken. We had never seen them before. While we were both serving them all night we got to know them better. They both got to like us and treated us with respect, not like the other customers. We both felt wanted and respected.

While I was sitting there listening to all this, my imagination was running wild. It was one of those things I didn't want to hear so I started hating hearing all this from her. Not just because I was empathetic and wished they had found love but it came to a period of just feeling down in the dumps just listening. Sometimes, it was hard to hear that and I wasn't too sure what to *say* most of time. But I wanted to hear more.

Day three

I returned to hear what was next to come. She continued,.... Because they liked both of us so much, we became casual friends and we started going out to other bars. These men could have been our fathers but we did not care, we just wanted the attention and they were giving it to us. These men were driving nice cars and they had money. They were businessmen. One of them owned an insurance company and the other was the owner of a funeral parlour (under-taker), and every so often we would go and visit them at their workplace and have lunch and drinks.

We were approaching sixteen, but we looked older, so we faked our age. These men were married and had their families. Even though we were friends, we were becoming their secret and extended family. We wanted to build our dreams and were looking for a better life because we did not have family that cared about us so we were hoping these men would give us a head start.

Your mother and I got pregnant by both of these men at the age of sixteen. And we were hoping that this would be the beginning of our life. We felt that passion and a deep sense of fulfilment as we were now pregnant and we felt we were growing up to be ladies with rich men. At first we were scared to tell them and were in doubt of having an abortion. In those days how do you go ahead with such a thing as abortion? There were no clinics and we were afraid because of our age as people would be asking lots of questions but as the months came along we had to let them know.

As they liked us so much, we felt that they were falling in love with both of us. It felt like romance and love. When I first broke the news, the fella I was with got very upset. He left in a temper. I had never seen him like this before. He said 'what do you want me to do'? His anger had swallowed his reason. He was wearing tight shoes with hard soles that were worn down unevenly because he had a funny way of walking, and we both heard those footsteps as he was making his way to his car.

I sat there crying my eyes out, thinking what I was going to do. Your mother heard and saw everything that was happening and she came and put her arms around me and said 'It will be OK.'

We both got up and started walking for a whole day and night until we came to the last of our strength. We saw a little house behind some gates, so we both decided that we were going to use it that night to sleep. We climbed over the gate and when we got to the house, it was locked so we couldn't get inside. We continued to walked into another field and across to the bank of a narrow river and we lay down there beneath a willow tree.

That night as we were lying there I was so tired but I couldn't sleep. I sat up and said to your mother, 'I've got this awful pain just here', pointing to the left side of my tummy. She looked at me and made a face, as she was afraid for me and what was happening. I then started to cry and said 'It feels like something's really wrong.' Woozily noting that it was in the early hours of the morning, it was a bit dark and no one knew we were there, she asked what kind of pain it was. With the tears flowing down my face I said 'like something's biting into me and won't stop.'

'Hold on', she said blearily, 'I will try and get help.' Bearing in mind that your mother was also pregnant and she could barely walk herself because her feet were swollen from all the walking we did earlier, she got up and went somewhere. I could not see where she went as it was very dark but she brought me back some water. Only heaven knows where she got that water from, but because I was so desperate I drank it and hoped that it would help in some way. As I was drinking the water, she was clutching my hand and waiting for the ache to subside.

After an hour, I was sitting up in real distress. I said 'It's getting worse now, really nasty. We may have no choice than to go to the hospital'. So we decided to walk again to the main road. Miraculously, as soon as we arrived at the main road, we saw a car and we stopped it and asked the driver to take us to the hospital. The driver saw how much pain I was in and he felt it was dangerous to leave us at the roadside while I was in so much pain.

When we arrived, the driver walked with us into the hospital as he wanted to make sure we were ok. The hospital was very busy but the doctor came and saw us straight away. As soon as I saw him, I felt so relaxed but also scared because of all the questions that I was expecting to come later.

The flurry of action made the pain subside, if only through distraction, and we both sat there while the doctor brought forms to be filled out, took my blood pressure and ran tests. A registrar poked a needle into my wrist and said, 'Does that hurt? Does that? How about that?' before concluding: 'Impressive. You have a very high pain threshold.'

They then took me to a ward and asked your mother to wait outside. Lying on that hospital bed I felt only 'discomfort' after such agony – an agony that was aggravated by fear that I now have to give birth to a child. The way I was feeling was 'it's like I've been attacked with a stapler; like having rabbits running up and down my spine'.

The nurses hooked my belly up to the monitor and ran a few tests. They concluded that the fluid was definitely amniotic, as suspected. I said 'this is really happening'. Later that evening the midwife came in and explained that labour would need to start very soon, because there's a high risk of infection after your water breaks. That evening on the 22nd September a baby girl was born a few weeks early.

While I was busy with my discomfort and agony, your mother was also having her baby few doors down the corridor and there you were born on the same day. Just a few minutes apart.

Listening to all of this and hearing all this for the first time, was giving me some sort of understanding of what was going on in these people's lives.

Day four

I returned for another visit. I needed to hear more. So she continued again by telling me: We both were young and now had the babies, not knowing how to bring them up. We tried to make contact with the fathers but they did not want to know anymore because it would break up their families. So we had to think quickly what to do next.

We both went back to my mother and she took us in for a while. When my mother saw me with this baby, she said 'whose child is that?' I said 'it's mine.' She looked at me, took the baby, laid the baby down on the bed, and then gave me a good beating of a lifetime. The whole community knew what a disgrace I was to the family. Your mother was sitting there thinking what will happen now.

We stayed there for about six months, but the situation was getting from bad to worse with my mother and your mother. Your mother had a temper and filthy mouth, and she wasn't scared to answer back. So it was not safe anymore to stay there.

We both decided one evening to take our babies and run away. I could not take my baby as she was sleeping in my mother's room. So we took you and we made a trip to your adopted mother and left you there. We both promised to come back for you. Of course, your mother was well prepared for the worst to come when we arrived. But funnily enough that did not happen. Your adopted mother accepted you and was happy to have you. Your adopted mother's husband was not happy about that. We left you there, and life was back to normal for us again.

While we were now in our twenties, your mother found another rich guy and she got pregnant again. This time it was a baby girl. Life was full of parties and fun, so again she did not make the time to look after that baby and because of all the drinking and smoking and the parties, the baby was born a few months early. That scared the life out of your mother so she took the baby and left her with your adopted mother. After seeing your baby sister and how tiny she was, I got scared and I had decided not to have any more children.

Life was getting harder and tougher, so we both decided to take a trip to the nearby country (Dutch). We got our passport, money and off we went. When we got to the port to board the ferry we met your adopted mother's niece there.

Your mother knew her, as they were living together for a while at your adopted mother. She herself was running away from a husband who was very abusive. She was trying to decide whether to stay or leave for a very long time, as she was feeling confused, uncertain, frightened, and torn. She was still hoping that her situation would have changed and was also afraid of how her husband would have reacted if he discovered that she and the three children were trying to leave. So she found at that moment that she was desperately wanting to get away and it was time to make a go for it as she did not want to hang on to that relationship anymore. She was even starting to blame herself for the abuse and felt weak and embarrassed because she stuck around in spite of it. What was her family was going to say?

She was also young in her late teens when she got pregnant with her first child and there she was trapped by confusion, guilt, or self-blame. The only thing that really mattered was her safety and her kids.

We all travelled together to start a new life. We stayed together in a small house we rented, and one by one we went and got ourselves our own places to live. But we kept in touch with each other.

Your mother met your sister's father and they lived together for many years. He started to take advantage of her because of her immigration papers and then she found out that he was gay. After a few years your mother fell pregnant.

He started to be abusive towards her after she confronted him about his sex life. She caught him having sex with a man in the house. She moved out and went and live with his mother for a while. She became afraid to stay in the house with him. As a police officer he always had his gun at home with him and he said to her that he was going to shoot her one day. That's why she packed her stuff and moved out and stayed at his mother's house.

When the baby was born, she moved back to his place with the baby hoping things would have changed. This was the first grandchild in the entire family. So everyone was very excited and full of joy that a new born came into the family and most importantly that this gay person now had a baby. This made everyone start to think, if he was gay or not or was he bisexual.

About six months later, he started to be abusive again towards your mother. She started to fear for her life and the unknown. It was getting a bit dangerous and the situation was getting unhealthy. She moved out again and this time she came and stayed with me for a while. The guy I was with at the time, did not approve, because your mother was a runaway wife with a child that belonged to a police officer, and he did not want any problems.

So your mother took your little baby sister back to our country to ask your adopted mother to look after her and your adopted mother's husband said no. She had to bring her back and left her with her father.

In my head while she was talking I was thinking everyone had been quiet around me. No one had said anything, not even my sister's father. There was a lot to take in and now I was seeing everything quite different because of the things she was talking to me about. I knew everyone had their good and bad times in life, but this was making me see these people differently.

Firstly, I was thinking about the things that was happening to me with this attitude of curiosity and self-exploration. Yes I was interested in the past to try to draw some conclusions about myself and this family.

This was leading me to learn more about myself. All this information I was hearing was making me think about what I needed to do and how I could change over time. This was helping me to really value myself and learn how to increase my problem solving skills. Not only did I know more about the past, but the calm reflection brought on by introspection helped me work through my problems.

This gave me a way to break out of the repetitive thinking about the past, and to extend my thinking into the present moment, and into the future. I started to think of it in terms of hope, optimism and positivity.

Day Five

In such a moment, I started to become filled with anxiety and my brain would start running in endless loops, asking numerous questions, criticizing my mother, questioning her worth and envisioning various responses in an attempt to alleviate her discomfort.

My anxiety started to decrease, thereby reinforcing myself and my brain that all this overthinking must be working. But, it never lasted long. Soon enough, another thought and feeling would surface and the cycle of deceptive brain messages would begin anew.

My self-worth, my future, all these families or something else, over-analysing in these repetitive ways was exhausting and rarely led to a productive and helpful outcome. Rather, I wasted time overthinking events, myself, my actions, people's intentions and thoughts, or repeatedly trying to plan for all potential future outcomes, even though most times none of those scenarios ever played out.

My initial brain-based thoughts, urges, emotional sensations, impulses and desires were at face value and I assumed they must be true. So I returned to hear more of what she had to say.

After leaving your baby sister with her father, your mother disappeared and did not tell anyone where she was. Everyone in our circle started to worry about where she was. Then one day after a few weeks I was at work and I got this phone call. It was your mother and she said 'I am now in England.' Your mother found some guy who helped her with her visa to go to England. How she did it I don't know. But we kept in touch for a while.

When someone who you loved like a sister leaves without a word, there is always a '*what if.*' There was always a question unanswered or something that was not said. We never kept secrets from each other.

113

We talked about everything. Most of the time I was thinking that she was alright and just couldn't believe she had moved to another country. But was she coming back? Was it my fault?

I've been there. It is not a beautiful experience. It is more painful especially if it was someone who you loved and grew up together with all your life. I lost a piece of my heart when I didn't get the chance to wish her good luck or to say goodbye. I realised I should have been more conscious of what was going on with her life. But, I had my own problems to deal with, and we both were there for each other.

Many of us or maybe not many, a few of us get too attached very quickly. When we met, we fell for each other almost unconsciously, without thinking. We saw each other as sisters. We were special people. When she left I found it difficult to move on. Asking why did she leave without me?

Your mother does not know that you are in this country. Your mother never told you that you had a sister. As a matter of fact you do not even know what your mother looks like. You have to find all of this for yourself. I have her last address where she was in England.

Listening to all of this I said to her 'I might be late knowing all of this, but it's not too late. But late enough to know that she has a son. Her first born. I was willing to hear all of this. I am glad that this has come out now, thank you.'

She found a photo of my mother and showed it to me. I was a bit excited to see what she looked like. Then came a photo of my biological father (who was rich) and she said 'you were the outside child. No one of that family knows that you existed.'

I got the address for my mother and I wrote her a letter explaining that I would love to see her and letting her know where I was and what my situation was with this family. I heard nothing for a while (about three weeks), then came a reply. She had moved where she was living in England, and it took a while for her to receive my first letter. I was happy and excited to get a reply.

The promise

After reaching out to my biological mother, I was hoping that she was happy to hear from me too. Little did she know that my life was soon to be consumed by these powerful feelings I was having. In a desperate attempt to fix her broken relationship with me I had to beg her to join her in starting a relationship that cold clear the path to a better future for both of us.

Definitely I was excited to meet her on that appropriate day when it came (whenever it was) and I was getting older every day and year and it would be nice to meet her. So I made that clear in one of my letters that I would like to see her face-to-face and start having that relationship we lost over the years and try to discourage a lack of communication between us. This was certainly a fascinating promise I made to her. However, the execution was somewhat lacking, hence the low star rating I was giving her at this point. I kept on keeping the communication going and said on every occasion how I was really looking forward to being part of such an amazing day when we can see each other, and how it would be one of those emotional days. I knew that her friend I spoke with would be happy for me and I had that incredible feeling knowing that her friend wanted me to succeed and make my life better.

Even though I hated the experience she been through in her life, I wanted her to know that she had me in her life now. She didn't know me from all the previous years, and I didn't even know her either, so I decided to reinvent myself and tell lies when people asked me about her. In the heat of the moment when I mentioned her name in conversation, it seemed like this family always had something bad and interesting to say. I knew that talking about her to the family would have started spreading to the other family members, and everyone would have something bad to say to me about her. She was well known to this family for a long time for so much of her life in that country.

Everyone has their baggage and everyone has their own characteristic qualities in them. I realised that some were bigoted and prejudiced, deceitful, and some had shameful behaviours, and intrusiveness. This family was saying all kinds of bad things about my mother maybe to discourage me from meeting with her. From my childhood I was left perplexed, isolated, and alone, dealing with a deep wonder as to whether I was really experiencing what I believed I was experiencing—and, if I did experience all that, why the people around me were reporting such different experiences.

From the time I knew myself and growing up from such a young age, when something difficult happened, I would look to others who were complete strangers for comfort and guidance. Most of them were always there for me, helping me work through the issue or helping me gain perspective. No matter what, these strangers had a positive outlook and some taught me to value the wonderful moments in life and how to persevere in difficult times.

As a child, one thing one of the elders would often say to me was, 'this too shall pass.' At first, I found this annoying. What I was dealing with seemed like the most important and difficult thing ever at the time. How would it ever be okay again? How would it get better? As I matured, I realised they were right. Life moves on and we all have a choice to move forward or chose to go back. I had always chosen to move forward.

My biggest personal challenge was when I was alone, it felt I had no one to talk to about my situation or my trouble and when I did found the courage to talk to someone, it was always a stranger. Most of the time it was so important to me and it became influential in all aspects of my life. The absence of a real parent was painful and more challenging than I had ever imagined. For years, I hated Mother's Day and Father's Day, as I did not have any biological parents who I could visit or who were a phone call away when I needed advice or wanted to share something special. It was a real sense of loss, something you can't understand unless you are living it.

I mentioned all of this in many letters to my mother. It seemed I was very repetitive in every letter I wrote to her. Sometimes it would be ages before she replied but I was satisfied so far with the communication.

I believed my mom was a very nice person who spent most of her adult life chasing the next person who would take care of her. She told me that she was now married with her second husband. I told her it would be nice to visit her very soon, as I was seeking to get away from this family and their situation.

We put a plan together by organising a date and the ticket was booked. I planned it very carefully because I wanted to have control over everything including when and what time to leave and did not let anyone know. I was determined to start rebuilding this fractured relationship with my mother. She said in one of her letters that she had built a good life where she was. I knew this relationship would have a lot of history, and more than its share of resentments. I had no judgment, as I don't know any of the details of her situation where she was. I knew where my boundaries were and I was willing to operate on that principle.

The only thing for me was to plan to run away from this family, without anyone knowing. No one would expect this from me. I wasn't a goody-goody, but I was trying to behave as a decent person. I was behaving as a characteristically stable and rational person, at least from the outside, so one would suspect anything.

The whole thing seemed strange and out of character to me in retrospect, but at the time it felt like the only solution to a series of problems with this family. There were little snippets of things which seemed to stick in the "what if" side of my brain and sometimes turned into a worry. There were always tensions rising within this family especially knowing that I was still a stranger in some eyes.

CHAPTER ELEVEN

The Highs and Lows

Loneliness

Looking after myself was something I knew since I was living and growing up with my adopted mother. I had learned to cook, clean, and look after myself and living with this family I was feeling a bit unwanted as if I could not do anything right in their eyes. There was no support from anyone who I could talk to in those days back in the eighties and the options were hard to access, and unavailable for a while.

As you may know, we all feel lonely from time to time. Feelings of loneliness were becoming very personal to me, and my experience of loneliness was becoming different. One of the common descriptions of my loneliness was the need for rewarding social contact and relationships of family that were not met. But soon I realised that loneliness was not always the same as being alone.

I had a choice, either to choose to be alone and live happily without much contact with other people, or find other people who were having the same lonely experience as me.

'One thing I've learned is the difference between feeling alone and feeling lonely - and how I can feel lonely in a crowd full of people, but quite peaceful and content when I was alone.'

This feeling lonely wasn't in itself a mental health problem, but the two were strongly linked. Having a mental health problem was increasing my chance of feeling lonely. It also had a negative impact on my mental health, especially when these feelings lasted a long time. It was increasing my risk of certain mental health problems, which included depression, anxiety, my low self-esteem, having a bit of trouble of sleeping and, it all came with stress.

For some people, certain life events may mean they feel lonely but for me it wasn't. I was not experiencing any sort of bereavement, changing of jobs, feeling any isolation from my co-workers or anything like that. It was the circumstances that I now knew was happening within the house I was now living in. Moving to a new country without a biological family, and hoping to find a new life with a new family, I really thought things were going to work out differently.

Maybe my expectation was a bit too high, and I was looking to belong to the group of people in this family and live with others from a similar background. But instead I started to experience some sort of discrimination and stigma because of the person I was. Not from the country, not speaking the language clearly, and my upbringing was far different what was happening there.

Loneliness had a very distressing feeling, something that would come and go or become more persistent. The loneliness I was experiencing was throughout my life, not just in later life. I had been feeling lonely for a while but I only noticed it more when the months passed as I was living with this family. There was not one way to effectively deal with loneliness but there were lots of different things that I did to help. I started to reach out and make new connections with others, and some were the best way to deal with the loneliness while others took advantage of it.

Making new friends near and far - I realised that friendships are like plants that need water I and I needed to invest time in maintaining them. I started to reach out to my friends, meeting up for chats (as in those days there was no such thing as social media). In some cases I felt that they were busy and won't have time for me, but in most cases, they really surprised me and they made an effort to connect.

Having those deep connections with close friends was important to me but brief exchanges with others was also having an impact on how I felt about myself. Simple things as saying hello to a neighbour, the shopkeeper or even the person at the bus stop.

I hated to be alone. This was not a periodic loneliness, it was not a loneliness that creeps up and puts a hand on your shoulder when you're at a party without a partner, and you suddenly miss that. This was not the type of loneliness that watches over you at night when you're alone. It's not even the loneliness that manifests when someone close to you dies, and you are left without their physical presence. No. This was a constant loneliness that accompanied my every waking – and sleeping – hour. It was the loneliness that arrests the blood flowing to and from my heart when I could share my deepest feelings, only to have them disregarded, disparaged or derided. It was the loneliness that sees myself craving physical contact so much that I will scoop up the odd smile sent in my direction, and try to turn it into a loving caress. Even if that's only in my mind.

It was the type of loneliness that, in order to combat it, I would try to ignore it. I would give away pieces of myself in silent exchange for acceptance. If I could be less of me and more of something else, then I will be accepted and therefore less lonely.

I've always enjoyed company, revelling in chat and laughter. But the hidden scorn of paranoia and insecurity could easily spoil the anticipated gladness of socialising and connecting. Talkative, engaging but quietly doubtful. Apprehensive about personal viewpoints on the basis that someone might not like me because of what I thought or what I said.

These experiences of depreciation and mindless punishment are just a few from many clouded moments of confusion and misunderstanding in my very being. However they have played a vital role in my eventual willingness to discover a grasp in managing doubt and fear that rises when life is interrupted.

Open and free

I didn't know why I all of a sudden had this thought, but I kept asking myself how it is that my life has changed as drastically as it had over the last year. How had I found this much happiness and joy for life? Why has it taken me so long to find it? And what did I do to deserve to have found it in the first place?

The truth is, it's because I decided to be open and free. The life of seclusion that I was living before wasn't providing me with any benefits, so to change my life, I knew that I needed to change my mentality.

How open am I? I'll be honest: I'm not a very open person. If I were a door, I would be locked most of the time. For various reasons, I have learnt over the years that I am suspicious and distrusting of others because of my past experiences. Due to my lack of trust, I am like a document that has a password-protected. I'm obsessed with guarding myself, to the point that I hesitate to let others check me out for themselves, narrowing my eyes and quickly replying, 'Why? What for?' when asked if I can lend or borrow something for a moment. This, I know, is a problem.

Being the type of person who is pretty closed emotionally and physically (most time people can see my body language!) is not healthy. In fact, it was very limiting for me. It hindered any relationships I had and it typically prevented me from starting new ones. The fact that I rarely opened my door, even a crack, for other people, is a problem and it definitely stood in the way of my happiness. For that reason, I've taken some time to think about how I could be more open with others. Just like being positive, this did not come easy for me. It was something I had to work at every day, but I think that outlining some tips to helped me do this.

Whether my door is generally wide open or typically shut tight, I think about all my situations in my life and whether I am more or less open. While I probably shouldn't tell every single person I meet every little detail of my life, I know and am still learning that it is not necessary to keep the door completely closed.

For me this one is key. The more I learned, the more I read about, the more I knew. The more I knew, the more likely it was that I would be able to relate to someone on some level and because I was always interested in learning new things and I loved to read, this one was pretty easy for me to want to do. I also liked watching the news and keeping up with current events. I would not be the person I am today if I hadn't learned to be open minded and learn from my mistakes and be willing to accept more connections along the way.

This one is also *really* important. Generally I had very closed body language. Folded arms. Crossed legs. Body angled away from the person I was speaking to. I tended to look around a lot when I was talking to others, mostly because I was uncomfortable or distracted by my own thoughts. I didn't smile nearly as often as I should. Smiling and using open body language made me appear much more open so I planned to work on this a lot.

As I mentioned before, I tended to be distracted very easily when it came to interacting with others. I was either thinking about what I want to say next or thinking about something else entirely. This was especially true when the conversation was not interesting to me. Either way, this did not help me to be open to others. This kept me focused on me, inside myself, and stopped me from connecting with other people. I had to work on listening better, I had to work a bit harder to be able to connect with others on a deeper level. I was also surprised by what I heard when I opened myself up to the words of others instead of staying trapped in my own little head.

Being open-minded was really tough sometimes. Like myself, most of us are brought up with a set of beliefs and values and, throughout our lives, we tend to surround ourselves with people who share the same values and beliefs. I found it a bit difficult when I was faced with ideas that challenge my own values and, though I may wish to be open-minded, I sometimes struggle with the act of it from time to time.

I tell you one thing that came out of my experience was realising that maintaining an open mind is a huge part of successfully manifesting the future I wanted. After all, I needed to learn how to be open to my own power of attraction, and open to potential opportunities that might not look quite as I expected. Having an open mind had given me the license to think more freely, and let my thoughts flow naturally. This led me to challenge old habits that no longer worked for me, and it began to trigger exciting new ideas or inspirational thoughts.

When my mind was open to new ideas, my worldview began to evolve. While this might mean holding on to many of the same beliefs, it also meant that I had the license to replace negative and limiting beliefs with positive ones that led to better results.

Being open meant that I had to hold nothing back. I had to learn to be open to new ideas, new adventures, and a life full of yes-es. But it also meant that I had to be open with not only my triumphs, but with my struggles as well. I was very afraid of failure. But as time went on and I got older I had to dissect failure piece by piece to learn from it, and I used what I had learned to guide myself towards a brighter future.

Being an "open person" meant many different things to me, maybe because I didn't trust anyone. This was a term I had learnt that had no set definition, but generally included some combination of friendliness, approachability, honesty, open-mindedness, tolerance, and personal authenticity. With the people around me I realised that open people tended to be more happy, charismatic, likable, and successful compared to people who were "closed off." While some people are open by nature, others can learn to be more open with practice and a little mindfulness.

To be honest I was that person that was closed off through deception. I had a habit of lying to everyone around me by telling them what I thought they wanted to hear. I used to close people off completely, since nobody knew who I really was. I have learnt and am still learning to try my best to be more open and do my best to be honest about myself and my opinions.

I have been more open to new perspectives, willing to question my thoughts and tried to think and act differently. I tried to stay attached to my emotions and my need to be right while fighting for my right to continue to do the right thing along with trying not to resist getting help and being more open to change. Suffering was inevitable in my journey. I experienced challenges as I was growing up. I have learnt strategies and developed beliefs that protected me when I was younger.

Learning to trust

Life can sometimes be a magical and mysterious journey. It's often hard to see the magic when we are struggling to keep our minds together with everything going on with our lives. Understanding what life is all about and how we experience things and learning to trust to move on to another level or another stage in life can be difficult.

Most times we mistakenly believe that we have to do it all ourselves. When we open up to something greater, we see that life is here to grant us our heart's deepest desires and most life-enriching experiences. All we have to do is take one step toward it.

One blind, trusting step. Life can take us to another plan when we least expect it. I had to learn to love myself, and redefined what success looked like. This was a journey into the mysteries of the universe and the great unknown. It was a chance for me to see the world through a new lens and create a significantly more magical and fulfilling life ... one simple, scary, and life-giving trust fall at a time.

My eyes betrayed my mind many times and the big tears rolled down my cheeks. I may have looked at certain people in my life and said 'you are the reason I don't have it in me to love or trust anyone, remember that.' In my heart my tone was sharp but my hands were trembling as I swiftly turned around and rushed off not wanting to hurt myself anymore in their presence.

I have learnt from an early age to have big ambitions so I could provide a high quality, dynamic education to build on my foundations. That way, I could be effective in society and have a positive outward look at myself, wherever and whatever I chose to do.

Most of the time I would make an assumption that would rely on and bolster my ability to trust people. In some cases if I needed help, I could turn to someone I was willing to trust. If I needed support, the person close to me would be there for me and happy to give it. I was willing be comforted and relieved by the support they were willing to give me. In contrast, the people I was exposed to who were not blood family and only caregivers were inconsistent. Sometimes they were a source of comfort and sometimes absent. I worried they won't be available or responsive at a time of need. In some cases I did not trust them to be present and was anxious about relying on them.

My life situation was very basic and I found over time, to learn how to trust people around me. I was always open to opportunities for collaboration, or for others to join in my projects, where my vision and values were aligned and where mutual benefits could be achieved. In some cases it was an opportunity for me and I saw it as a sort of empowerment.

Over the years I have learnt to rebuild trust after infidelity or intimate betrayal when I was given hope in a relationship. Intimate betrayal includes sexual betrayal, emotional betrayal, financial betrayal, relational betrayal, addiction betrayal, and physical abuse betrayal.

A child growing up, who had to learn the lessons that people close to them are reliable, can be trusted and will take care of them, goes out into the world with very different mental presentations and expectations about human interaction than a securely attached peer.

As someone who has felt first hand, the sting of betrayal, I know that it isn't always easy to trust. But I'd like to think that I'm still open to the possibilities of close relationship to offer more than just hugs and kisses.

I realised that I never let people in for fear they would let me down, make me feel small, or otherwise diminish me in some way. I kept people at a distance and this impacted my ability to have close, connected relationships. I used to think I had trust issues because I grew up in a family that was not biological (strangers) where things were not "psychologically safe" but I've come to realise there is more to it than that.

I have always struggled with trust issues thinking they were caused by something outside myself. I started to believe that trust was a matter of what other people did, how they treated you, or how they disappointed you. Maybe it was time for me to consider that perhaps my trust issues are more about me than other people.

Yes, people would sometimes disappoint me and yes, people would occasionally do malicious things but, in the end, I had to learn to get over it. I told myself I needed to move on from continuously licking the wounds so I could heal them and start living fully again.

As a child I was naturally trusting, sharing my thoughts, and my heart with abandonment. It wasn't until I realised I had to train myself to distrust the world and not talk to people who just didn't care about my problems, that I began to lose my innocence and belief in the inherent goodness of humanity.

There have been many occasions when a person was about to open a door for me, but I was so busy being independent that I opened it myself without even noticing their attempted act of kindness. I had to learn to trust, despite knowing I may get hurt. It is only by opening my heart that I could have flourishing relationships, see the opportunities around me, and begin to live a more fulfilled life. There were many times people let me down. I had to accept that they were imperfect beings and move on. Letting myself down, I could live with. This is where I think I got hung up. I didn't trust myself, and this actually made it impossible to trust other people.

Past to Present

Many people who start to look back on their past when they enter the second half of life, in particular, become immersed in memories as they recall both good and hard times. But such passive retrospection isn't enough. It will take time to do an interim accounting of your life, reflecting actively and intentionally on your past, with an intention to design your period of completion with a new mind set and new goals.

As the years pass and the seasons change in accordance with the cycles of nature, it is only me who gives meaning to those changes, and only me who chooses renewal. Unless I reflect on what I have learned through the past years and on how I will apply those lessons to my future life, aging another year won't make me any wiser.

What you have read about my past has been scary, sad, painful, and mostly full of memories I can't forget. Some were good, some bad. What would have happened if I did things differently that one day?

Growing up, I remember my situation as extremely chaotic. I felt I had little time to develop my own unique perspective and voice when I was very young. Even as I can remember from a very young age, I remember doing chores to help out at home. However, this situation did foster some positive aspects of my character in what I am today. I learned to be mature at an early age and gained a sense of competence because of my responsibilities and what I had to do.

Over the years I trained myself that if conflict is not fully resolved, the problems will always be there for a long time. However, as a child I learnt to carry those unresolved issues into the next stage, and this helped me not to truly mature. During this stage and over the years I had gained a sense of competence as a caregiver.

I was forced to learn quickly with a new culture, language and customs. I was taught to be independent and work hard. Returning to college, with family that was not biological was a challenge but I was able to achieve or near enough complete my long time goal and try to make a better life with something I had learned over the years.

I also taught myself to put the needs of others before my own. I feel that I did not learn to value my own, legitimate desires to an adequate degree as a young child and have only recently acquired a true sense of worth.

Life from an early age helped me to find meaning and value in my experiences. This led to a greater sense of meaning, which contributes to happiness in whatever way you look at it. Everything that has come my way growing up, shows the challenges I have overcome, and the personal strengths that allowed me to do so.

In life there are three main parts: the past, the present, and the future. Each part is crucial to the life we all live until this day. Without a past there can be no future, and vice versa. For this reason I believe it is important sometimes to reflect upon the past in an attempt to create the most beneficial present and future. Every word in this book is my way of reflecting upon my past and pondering what my present and future may hold. My past has been defined less by what I have done, and more by what others have done to me.

The past dictates who I am, but I am determined about what I want to become. Putting pen to paper, helps and explains why I am so successful in my present, only because of my efforts and hard work in the past. My past was the key to my present. I believe that the system of change defines "what I am" and it is because one moment is not the same as another that I was able to feel and experience many different things. Every experience taught me a lesson for a better life.

No one knows what the future looks like but we all know what the present is, and how it would describe our life and who we are now. The question would be, how do you differ from your past self? What are your strengths now? What challenges are you going to be faced with ahead?

In my younger days I was living in the present moment. Learning how to live in the present moment is not always an easy thing to do. I have got caught up in my past with things that I have done, people I have hurt psychologically and the self-pity that came along with living the life of a sex object or even an addict. While growing up into adulthood, I have come across many people that have never been able to leave their past and are never able to live in the present moment.

There are many ways I could look back over my life. I could divide my life into many units, bringing my mind to what were the important things which occurred in each of those time periods. Or I could think about what happened in each stage of my life that was meaningful too.

In a nutshell, I felt then that I was not loved in any of the places where I lived and if I wanted to be loved by my adopted family, I needed to follow the rules. I thought love was conditional on good behaviour. I was wrong. Maybe I was loved in all places though the expression of it wasn't clear to me at that time.

Life can seem confusing sometimes, especially with the position you take as you look at the mirror. It can just be a shiny tool to tweak the physical appearance or the mirror can also be used as way of building a powerful self-image and developing a strong sense of self trust.

We create a network of family and friends from time to time. Some of them can be good sources and some are there to be a disruption in your life which can affect the network status you created in the first place. Sometimes there will be times when you have to reconnect and disconnect so you can retune yourself.

When you start thinking about a situation or a problem you may be having and you come to a conclusion that you think is rational and true, you may have also recognised some conclusions or answers that are "untrue" or incorrect. These are valuable because often, the answers aren't in simple black and white. They may be among shades and hues of grey and other colours. You should compare an untrue conclusion, and a true conclusion in a line of thought and then try to see whether you can make sense out of any answer to be found between them. It may be a better way or not. Regardless, it will help to make you a more accepting and understanding individual.

Our life is under our full control, and no one else's! After all, only you know what's best. Get in tune with the sense of trust you have in yourself, turn your full attention to your mission in life and to your vision of what your realised dream will look like. Reach out to people who make you feel good and who know your true self. So ask yourself this, if you could change one thing about your life, what would it be?

CHAPTER TWELVE

Life is what you make it

Life is like a train ride. You are born into this world very innocently and people take care of you. You learn the things of life as you get older. We all learn to talk, walk, and learn the right path you need to go along with a bit of help.

There are accidents and there are delays. At certain stops there are surprises. Some of these will translate into great moments of joy; some will result in profound sorrow.

When we are born and we first board the train, we meet people whom we think will be with us for the entire journey. Those people are our parents, but sadly, this is far from the truth ... Our parents or adopted parents are with us for as long as we absolutely need them. They too have journeys they must complete. We live on with the memories of their love, affection, friendship, guidance and their ever presence.

We are like someone on a train, we meet other people, and it seems that we are all seemingly going to the same destination, but based on their belief in you or their belief that the train will get them to their desired destination. We will all stay on the ride and some will get off somewhere during the trip. As we continue life's journey, some of the people we meet can and will get off at any stop. Just know that where people get off is more of a reflection on them, than it is on you.

There are others who board the train and who eventually become very important to us, in turn. These people are our brothers, sisters, friends and acquaintances, whom we will learn to love, and cherish. Some people consider their journey like a jaunty tour. They will just go merrily along. Others will encounter many upsets, tears, or losses on their journey and some will linger on to offer a helping hand to anyone in need.

There will be a few people in your life that will make the whole trip with you. There are those who believe in you, accept that you are human with feelings and that mistakes will be made along the way. They believe that you will get to your desired destination, (maybe together or separately) no matter what.

We have to learn in life to be very grateful for the people that join us in our journey for good reasons or bad ones. The good ones are rare and when you find one, don't let go of them - ever. Be blessed for the ones who get on at the worst stops when no one is there. Remember those good people, they are special. Always hold them dear to your heart. But be very wary of people sneaking on at certain stops when things are going well and acting like they have been there for the whole ride. They will be the first to depart. There will be ones who secretly try to get off the ride and there will be those that very publicly will jump off. Don't pay any heed to the defectors. Pay heed to the people that are still on the trip with you. They are the important ones. If someone tries to get back on the train - don't be angry or hold a grudge, let them. Just see where they are around the next hard turn.

I found these beautiful words of a poem on the internet. I do not know the source of where it came from but I think it sums it up nicely

THE TRAIN OF LIFE

At birth, we boarded the train of life and met our parents, and we believed that they would always travel by our side. However, at some station, our parents would step down from the train, leaving us on life's journey alone.

As time goes by, some significant people will board the train: siblings, other children, friends, and even the love of our life.

Personally, I know I'll be sad to make my final stop ... I'm sure of it! My separation from all those friends and acquaintances I made during the train ride will be painful. Leaving all those I'm close to will be a sad thing. But then again, I'm certain that one day I'll get to the main station only to meet up with everyone else. They'll all be carrying their baggage ... most of which they didn't have when they first got on this train. I'll be glad to see them again. I'll also be glad to have contributed to their baggage ... and to have enriched their lives, just as much as they will have contributed to my baggage and enriched my life.

We're all on a train ride together. Above all, we should all try to strive to make the ride as pleasant and memorable as we can, right up until we each make the final stop and leave the train for the last time.

Life gives us all the opportunity for a new adventure, a new challenge. Let us set our goals and go for it. Be persistent. Trust in God; trust in Life, Trust in yourself.

Learning to have an open mind and truly understanding the meaning of life sounds like it isn't anything an ordinary mortal should be doing – or would get very far by doing. There are a small selection of people who might be equipped to take on the task and discover the answer in their own lives, but such ambition isn't for most of us.

I believe that meaningful lives are for extraordinary people: great saints, artists, scholars, scientists, doctors, activists, explorers, national leaders ... If ever we did discover the meaning, it would, we suspect, in any case be incomprehensible. We just have to always acknowledge that we are in the background, operating with a remarkably inconsequential perspective on the meaning of life.

In our prediction of how we want things to go, expectations can seem harmless. But not always. Low expectations can mean you underachieve in life or maybe let others manipulate you. And what about high expectations? In a world focused on success and ambition, they can seem exemplary and unreachable.

In life it's often a learned habit. You might have grown up, with a parent who demanded the best from you or others who had tantrums when things did not go their way. But life inevitably throws curve balls. So trying to force an unrealistic outcome from everything leads to being disappointed. Why is having a high expectation so important to reaching our goals and accomplishing our dreams? I mean, couldn't we just put our heads down and work towards an objective without an inflated sense of whether it's going to work out or not?

If you're working to become a better person, live healthier or hoping to make a change, then phrases like "go big or go home" or "stretch yourself" often get tossed around by well-meaning friends, family, and even the people you have to work with.

How many times in our life have we experienced hurt, disappointment, anger, or stress, from the difference between our imagination and reality? We're very creative creatures and when we set out to do things, we always expect that everything will turn out exactly the way we want.

Many people have discovered that the improvement of life was due to the different way that we learn as we grow older. Compared to the others, the "bloomers" were given feedback, allowed more time to see their mistakes, and generally received more smiles, nods, and gestures of approval. But unfortunately some don't, they just have to learn the hard way on their journey.

I have come close to falling a couple of times. Sometimes I was scared, which was good for me as it kept me sharp. I had no safety lines, no hard hats, and no nets - NOTHING. I have learnt to build bridges. I have been around many people in my life. Some people I worked with and some people I came across in my journey of life had no schooling at all. They could hardly read or write but most of them thought I was some highly educated person. I always offered to help the best way I could to all. Especially those with behaviour problems that impeded their academics. I was there at the right time at the right place to offer my help by giving them support and helping them develop better habits. It seemed I was a problem solver and maybe they saw I had the skills, social skills, conflict resolution skills, and many other proactive ways to help to better handle their own behaviour and improve their learning environment.

Everybody wants to be on the mountaintop, but unfortunately not everyone can be at the top and some of us have to be at the bottom. But I know, mountaintops are rocky and cold. There is no growth on the top of a mountain. Sure, the view might be great, but what's a view for? A view just gives us a glimpse of our next destination and our next target. But to hit that target, we must come off the mountain, go through the valley, and begin to climb the next slope. It is in the valley that we slog through the lush grass and rich soil, learning and becoming what enables us to understand life's next stage.

Life is not a long series of mountaintop experiences. Life is a long walk in the valley with an occasional trek up the side of the mountain for a breath of fresh air. Then, it's back to work at the bottom.

Why is it so hard sometimes and if not most times to be committed to the small things? Yes … in most cases they're less exciting, less pressing, and often it feels like there's less reward. But they're worth it. Our hard work in the valley pays off when we get to see the incredible views from the top. How can we maintain our calling in the midst of all this?

I have learned that I should always begin by showing myself that I can make a difference in the world. I will choose to pick one single thing that needs fixing and figure out how I can carve out the time, talent and resources from my life to get it done.

Today the sense of feeling deeply rooted, deeply centred and able to handle anything is a gift.

I think we've all had bratty, entitled moments, no matter how much money we grew up with or didn't have or how successful we became when we grew up. Maybe there was a time where we threw a tantrum when our parents or adopted parents only let us buy one thing instead of two, or maybe we bragged with our friends about our parents landing a high-paying corporate job while demeaning folks were "flipping burgers" at fast-food chains.

Regardless, entitlement can come from anyone of any age, generation, background, or class. It can also come in various forms and intensities. Sometimes, so-called entitled mind sets and behaviours are not considered entitled in the eyes of others. Meanwhile, there are other cases where it's clear that entitlement is present.

But nevertheless, we often assume that those who grew up wealthy are automatically spoiled, self-centred, and unappreciative. Heck, we've seen rich brats in movies but also in real life. As for me I had the opportunity to see that side of rich and spoilt people once in my life and I have witnessed exactly what being spoiled can do to a child, and believe you me it is not pretty.

While there are surely very well privileged people out there who are grateful for what they have and don't ask for a lot, it's still clear that others have completely let money go to their heads to the point where they not only want anything and everything but can't seem to understand what "normal" life is like for the average person, and maybe take advantage of others.

Yes I have experienced some folks who have lost the sense of what it means to be thankful, respectful, and empathetic towards others, all because growing up with money or nice possessions has warped their mind. That's the reason they say, "Money is the root of all evil," which is more relevant than ever before.

What helped me was to start making the right choices, I needed to begin empowering myself with solid information about my options, and then learn what was available to me.

It's easy to assume best outcomes for myself and not spend time thinking about the "what if" moments in life. After all, who wants to think about the things that could go wrong? Yet when it comes to having confidence, it means more than just going for the short-term goals when the long-term goals were ahead. It means putting my safety nets in place so that if something *does* go wrong, it doesn't derail my plan. I had to learn to be prepared for the worst, provided I had peace of mind, which can benefit all aspects of my life.

It's no secret that things can go wrong. I have seen it when natural events have caused people to abandon everything and possibly lose much of what they had. And while it's already a horribly sad situation, for many, events like this can be a heavy burden on themselves and affected their families as well—causing additional strain at an already difficult time in their lives.

Resilience was my ability to adapt and cope with difficult things that happen in life. It's what helped me to bounce back and to keep going no matter how hard things were. Often I was surprised by the extent of my resilience and how I was able to cope with much more than I had realised. But as a person I knew I was hardwired to be able to cope with all sorts of things that happened in my life and I had a natural resilience that kicked in when I needed it.

I was taking each day as it came. Sometimes I was thinking too far ahead and trying to deal with everything that was going on in my life at once and that was a bit overwhelming. I needed to focus on the here and now, breaking things down into manageable chunks and focusing on getting through each day and hour by giving myself small achievable goals and rewarding myself when I was able to complete them. Getting through tough times happens minute by minute. I had learned how to do it and just kept going.

Inspirational

Our motivations have an amazing ability to change the way we feel about life. This is why I find them so interesting and crucial on our paths to success.

Too many people go to work wishing they didn't have to. They wake up tired and spend their day tired. Sometimes our hearts bleed when we hear certain things about what others are saying or doing in their life. Which is why I decided to do something about it.

Over the years I was and am still learning "Be yourself", everyone and everything else is already taken. You have to dance like there's nobody watching and be the change that we wish to see in the world. No one can make us feel inferior without our consent. We all need to live as if we were to die tomorrow. Darkness cannot drive out darkness: only light can do that.

You see, the way we think and feel about ourselves, includes our beliefs and expectations about what is possible for us, and determines everything that happens.

We're living in the most amazing time in human history and yet every day I see people who don't know it and don't feel it. We have modern plumbing, healthcare, abundant food, rapid travel, access to anything you'd ever want to know and learn available for free in most places if you want to look for it. In many ways, we have the ability to do just about anything we'd want to and yet, *something holds us back*.

When we change the quality of our thinking, we can change the quality of our life, sometimes instantly. Just as positive words can make someone smile or a well-timed humorous quote can make someone laugh, our thoughts react to the world in real-time.

I can't predict what I am going to think in any given situation. My thoughts and feelings determine my actions and determine the results I get. It all starts with my thoughts and I have found that inspirational words are a quick way to retune my thinking.

As the years went by I kept a few uplifting excerpts and positive proclamations on hand. If I ever noticed my energy or my spirit beginning to drop, I simply recited an inspirational and uplifting quote to quickly boost my mood. And most of the time it would be a verse from the bible because God's word is always true.

There are a lot of things which I know can provide inspiration, and I have seen other people accomplish great things, seen other people overcome adversity, heard inspirational words from great people and even the beauty of God's nature can remind us just how lucky we are to be alive.

I found and like this quote

"You've have to dance like there's nobody watching, Love like you'll never be hurt, Sing like there's nobody listening, And live like it's heaven on earth." by William W. Purkey

I had to focus more on my opportunities than what was worrying me. I had to feel more of the abundance around me, instead of my limitations. I knew there were better things ahead and I had to start living my out dream today instead of waiting for something to happen way off in the distant future.

For me, nothing is more inspiring than learning from real people who are manifesting their dreams. From inspiring people I have come across in real life or from what I have seen and who have found ways of turning obstacles into opportunities. Those people had figured out ways to be resourceful when they lacked resources, focused more on persistence and dedication than excuses and reasons why something won't work. I knew that there was some awesome abundance all around me when I started to focus on it.

I like to get my energy from positive people. The truth is that my energy comes from what I focus on. If I start to focus on what I'm worried about, then my energy will be worry-based. If my focus is on gratitude and opportunity, my energy will be ... pretty awesome! If there's one thing I learned from it is to master fully what I have learnt and that will be my focus.

There will be a thrilling surprise waiting for me. That is an awesome thing because I knew I was going to achieve my goals and get what I most wanted in my life.

What I have learnt, it is that our lives can be turned upside down overnight. While there isn't much any of us can do to prepare for it, it is important to look to the future to see what you can do to prepare for other life-changing events that may arise in the future.

I know that change can feel scary and uncertain but it can be a really positive thing, because I have experienced it. I try my best to be curious and open to it. Sometimes things don't work out as planned and things can happen in life that bring about change that I didn't expect or even want. However, that change also brought new opportunities. As much as I might have wanted and craved security and predictability, I realised that life doesn't always work like this but by being open to change and expecting it, I knew I was willing to grow my adaptability and resilience.

Taking care of myself physically and emotionally was really important and I often forgot to do this, especially in the tough times. However it's when things got tough that it was even more important to look after myself as no one was going to do it for me. I did my best to start eating properly, exercising, socialising and trying hard to get some rest, which was the key to resilience and being able to cope. As tempting as it is to neglect these things, I did my best to nourish and support myself.

My mind was very easily taking me down a rabbit hole of negative thoughts, unhelpful thinking and fear. It was easy to get caught up in this thinking but my thoughts did not control me. I practiced trying to recognise my thoughts as being 'just' thoughts and tried to step outside of them even for just for a few moments. I found meditation and mindfulness was helpful to do this. My thoughts did not control me and sometimes my mind could feel tortured but I chose not to succumb to this. Forcing myself to recognise that my thoughts were running away from me was a really good place to start. Even if I could only step outside them for a few seconds to begin with, the more I practised, the easier it became.

ACKNOWLEDGEMENT

Appreciation and Express Gratitude

Yesterday I felt I was sinking into a tub full of warm mud. Today the sense of feeling deeply rooted, deeply centred and able to handle anything is a gift. All of my events and experiences have triggered changes that came very quickly when I was running in circles trying to figure out my life, not knowing I would be affected years down the line. Negative noise surrounded me as a teenager but as I got older I felt more and more grounded. And I know now that I can handle anything.

Hanging out with people in the past and listening to what they had to say, made me the person I am today. A few things grounded me, like knowing what a real family should look like and being able to clear my mind and being able to control my thoughts. I have appreciated that whenever I felt as though the world was spinning out of control. I would sit down, plant my feet solidly on the ground and close my eyes. I focused my attention on one part of my body after another for a few minutes. Then I would open my eyes, stand up and take a long stretch. It really helped me to feel the calmness inside and ready to restart the day.

These words of appreciation I am using are because I feel gratitude towards everyone in my life growing up. I cannot give you a gift or a favour. I wish you were alive, but I know in my heart you were a good and excellent parent toward me and you will always be in my heart. But these are some simple words of appreciation.

I want to recognise the value of the upbringing I have received in the short time my adopted mother spent with me and her contribution to my life. I am very sorry that I was not able to be with you to the end.

I am also giving thanks as part of my gratitude to the minister who had been there as a father and pastor to me, teaching and planting the spiritual seed so I could practice that important impact on my personal well-being.

I am deeply grateful to all who had a part to play in my life growing up. I am indebted to all who I have learnt from. I would also like to express the deepest appreciation to my sister's family especially her father.

Make focusing on gratitude a daily practice. Take the time to say "I have my health or I have a loving relationship". It will change your brain chemistry and allow you to move forward on solid ground.

I realised that it's true enough that all children of unloving and disengaged mothers have common experiences. The lack of maternal warmth and validation warps their sense of self, makes them lack confidence in or be wary of close emotional connections, and shapes them in ways that are both seen and unseen.

Keep looking in the mirror, receive and accept the signals, and keep moving on.

Mark Twain said: *"The two most important days in your life are the day you are born and the day you find out why."*

One is obvious. The other?

Jackie Robinson said: *"A life is not important except in the impact it has on other lives"*

These are two of the most powerful quotes I've ever read, and I try to live by both every day. I believe I was born to help build a more "likeable" world for myself, my family, and those who I affect through my writing, speaking, teaching and leading. I believe I was born to help motivate myself and others to become more transparent, authentic leaders who put others' needs first.

Why were you born? What is your purpose in life?

If you know the answers to those two questions, you're off to a great start, and I'll simply suggest that you remind yourself of the answers every day.

Instead of looking for influence from others and the world just look in the mirror. If you're not sure yet, it's never too late - or too early to figure it out.

There must be a purpose in life which can help people of all ages and backgrounds to determine their calling which can be well-suited for those of you who observe their faith. Life can be or can bring you on a journey both inward and outward.

"It is an absolute human certainty that no one can know his own beauty or perceive a sense of his own worth until it has been reflected back to him in the mirror of another loving, caring human being."
—John Joseph Powell, The Secret of Staying in Love

Once you start reading, it is so hard to put down!

If you're a seventies baby, you know what life was like before the internet and cell phones existed. But, real talk: You were probably too busy listening to New Kids on the Block and picking out the most colourful trapper keeper to care. If that sounds like your childhood, you'll totally relate to all of these memories, too.

Come to think of it, growing up in the seventies, eighties, and the nineties was not easy, but I did not know any better. Everyone used all that we had especially in a third world country. We got through life without the internet at all. Try living in a time when an Apple wasn't something you spent your entire allowance and existence on, but something you left on your teacher's desk.

If you needed to get somewhere back then, you had to send messages from your brain down to your legs. Your legs then engaged in a motion-based phenomenon known as 'walking.' Many people who grew up in those years didn't set foot in a car until they bought one.

Perhaps the weirdest thing about those years was its strict

adherence to the concept of time. If you wanted to meet your mates down at the video arcade at a certain time, you were forced into doing this bizarre thing where you all agreed to meet at that time, and then when that time came around, you all turned up at that time. It really was mind-boggling behaviour.

Lightning Source UK Ltd.
Milton Keynes UK
UKHW010628161020
371702UK00001B/64